About the author

Linda Parker has taught History for 20 years, but has now changed course to continue writing and to study for a PhD at Birmingham University. Her main areas of interest are 20th Century Military and Church History. She is a member of the Western Front Association. She was born and educated in Wales, but now lives in Oxfordshire. She enjoys hill walking and anything to do with Polar exploration. She is the daughter of a former Territorial Army Chaplain, a fact which has encouraged her in the research for this, her first book.

D1386208

THE WHOLE ARMOUR OF GOD

Anglican Army Chaplains in the Great War

Linda Parker

Foreword by Professor Gary Sheffield

Helion & Company Ltd

This Book is dedicated to my father, The late Revd Haydn Moses,
Territorial Army Chaplain 1956-1969

Helion & Company Limited
26 Willow Road
Solihull
West Midlands
B91 1UE
England
Tel. 0121 705 3393
Fax 0121 711 4075
Email: info@helion.co.uk
Website: www.helion.co.uk

Published by Helion & Company 2009
Designed and typeset by Farr out Publications, Wokingham, Berkshire
Cover designed by Farr out Publications, Wokingham, Berkshire
Printed by Cpod, Trowbridge, Wiltshire

Text © Linda Parker
Photographs © as individually credited within the book

Front cover image: A chaplain assisting in bringing in the wounded, La Boiselle, Amiens
Road, July 1916. (IWM Q721)
Rear cover image: Chaplain decorating an altar, preparing for a service. (IWM Q11041)

ISBN 1-906033-42-2

British Library Cataloguing-in-Publication Data.
A catalogue record for this book is available from the British Library.

For details of other military history titles published by Helion & Company Limited
contact the above address, or visit our website: http://www.helion.co.uk.

We always welcome receiving book proposals from prospective authors.

Contents

List of Illustrations

Key:
IWM – Imperial War Museum, London
RAChD Archives – Royal Army Chaplains Department Archives, Amport House

Foreword

It is fair to say that Anglican chaplains (padres) of the First World War have had a bad press. They have been depicted as unpopular ineffectual clergy who proved irrelevant to the needs of their flock in the trenches (often compared unfavourably with their Roman Catholic counterparts), or as men who compromised their spirituality by being 'one of the boys' and engaging in 'holy grocery', handing out cigarettes and the like; or of being inappropriately bellicose men who urged men into battles that they themselves did not have to endure.

In recent years historians have begun to question this version, and a rather different picture has emerged; the seminal work of my University of Birmingham colleague Dr Michael Snape has been particularly influential in this respect. Such revisionism is part of a pattern whereby our views of many aspects of the British army of the First World War, from the generalship of Field Marshal Sir Douglas Haig to minor infantry tactics have been transformed by scholarship in recent years. Like so much of what 'everyone knows' about the First World War, the traditional portrait of Anglican padres turns out to have been based on a mishmash of half truths, myths and prejudice. I have not been surprised by this revisionism. For many years I suspected that there was something amiss with the older version. What I knew of men like the Rev. E.P. St John, padre of the 22nd Battalion Royal Fusiliers, simply did not square with this negative picture, which has been perpetuated by some modern ecclesiastical historians who have shown little sympathy for the situation in which Anglican chaplains of the First World War found themselves. Perhaps a pacifistic dislike for the very idea of men of God participating in the war effort, especially a war that is (wrongly) believed to be 'futile', lies at the heart of modern criticisms.

Now Linda Parker has added her voice to the debate by writing this fascinating and important book on Anglican chaplains. The story that emerges is richer and more complex than the simplistic narrative of which we have heard so much. Crucially, she judges chaplains by the standards of their own time, not ours. Her achievement is to bring compelling evidence that, in her words, padres 'were simply men of God in the maelstrom of war endeavouring to bring God to the lives of the men in the trenches in whatever way they could'. She brings to life men such as William Drury and Harold Spooner, weaving their stories into the context of the brutal reality of life on active service in the First World War, demonstrating real understanding and insight in the process.

This book stands as an often moving testimony to the difficulties and sacrifices of a group of very human clergy, of various shades of churchmanship, far from perfect but striving to carry out what they saw as God's will in the midst of an appalling human situation, balancing spiritual with physical ministrations. As Linda Parker rightly comments, 'If Jesus could heal the sick and provide food for the five thousand as well as proclaiming God's kingdom then surely that was their job also'. She makes the case that Anglican padres of the First World War have been harshly treated by history. Those of us who call ourselves Christians, especially if we are Anglicans, should honour their memory.

Gary Sheffield
Professor of War Studies
University of Birmingham
Holy Week, 2008

Acknowledgements

I would like to acknowledge the support and advice given over several years by Mr David Blake, curator of the Royal Army Chaplains' Department Museum at Amport House and for permission given by him to quote from the papers of the Very Reverend H W Blackburne DSO MC and the *Journal of the Royal Army Chaplains' Department*.

I am indebted to Gary Sheffield who has provided advice and support and kindly written the Foreword.

I am grateful to Mr Ken Osborne of the Church Missionary Society for granting permission to quote from the papers of Bishop L.H. Gwynne and to the staff of the Special Collections Department at The University of Birmingham Library for providing access to Bishop Gwynne's papers.

I would like to thank Mrs Dorothy Hood, Mr A.R. Spooner and the relatives of Canon T. Rogers for permission to use copyright material held in the Imperial War Museum's Department of Documents. Every effort has been made to trace the copyright holders of the papers of the Revd Mervyn Evers, the Revd E.C. Crosse and the Revd L. Jeeves. The author and the Imperial War Museum would be grateful for any information which might help to trace those whose identities or addresses that are not currently known. Thanks are due to the staff of the Imperial War Museum for providing access to their document collection and the staff of the photographic section for permission to use photographs from the Imperial War Museum photograph archive.

Invaluable support and advice on layout, proofreading and references has been given by Ann Stevens who deserves much thanks for her vast supplies of time and patience. Thanks also to Elizabeth Hall for her help with images.

The writing of this book would have not have been possible without the unending and unfailing support of my husband Nigel who provided the inspiration for the book and has encouraged me at all times.

Finally, I must thank Helion and Company, particularly Duncan Rogers, for the enthusiasm shown for *The Whole Armour of God* and for the support given during its preparation.

Abbreviations

ADS   Advanced Dressing Station
BEF   British Expeditionary Force
CO   Commanding Officer
DHQ   Divisional Headquarters
DSO   Distinguished Service Order
GOC   General Officer Commanding
HQ   Headquarters
MC   Military Cross
MO   Medical Orderly
RAMC   Royal Army Medical Corps
SCF   Senior Chaplain to the Forces
VC   Victoria Cross
YMCA   Young Men's Christian Association

Introduction

On 22 February 1919, the Army Chaplains' Department received the accolade of becoming the Royal Army Chaplains' Department in recognition of what the King described as 'the splendid work which has been performed by The Army Chaplains' Department.'[1] At that point in its history it was deemed to have performed well in the war and played a useful role in its ministry to the troops. Subsequently, along with other groups such as the generals, in the general disenchantment and iconoclasm of the 1920s and 1930s, the army chaplains came in for much criticism. Famous literary figures who had been involved in the war such as Siegfried Sassoon and Robert Graves, whose books became bestsellers after the war, criticised the Anglican chaplains, in particular, for cowardice and incompetence. However, an examination of contemporary evidence written by chaplains and generals, officers and men of the army during the war uncovers a different story.

The Great War was to present the Army Chaplains' Department with challenges and difficulties on an unprecedented scale. The role of the army chaplain had been formalised since the Royal warrant of 1796. Their performance in the Crimean War had resulted in an increase in their establishment strength, and during the Boer War, the expansion of their role had resulted in the Chaplain's Department becoming an integral part of the fighting forces.

At the outbreak of war in August 1914 the establishment strength of the department was 117, from all denominations but with the vast majority, 89, being Anglican. The department was to grow in strength until in 1918 there were 3,475 chaplains, 1,985 of whom were Anglican.[2] The administrative structure was minimal and certainly not up to the vast strains that the war would shortly put upon it. Who could have predicted in August 1914 the ways in which the numbers of army chaplains would grow, and how their role would change as the war progressed? By November 1918, 166 chaplains had died as a result of war and 3 had won the VC. Many had been decorated for bravery, Anglican chaplains alone earning 37 DSOs and 205 MCs and Bar.[3]

The Anglican Church and its clergy had some hard decisions to make at the outbreak of war. The question of whether the clergy should join up as combatants or non-combatants was swiftly resolved by clear guidance from the Archbishop of Canterbury, Randall Davidson, but many Anglican clergy felt the opposing pressures of wanting to join up as temporary chaplains and the need of their parishes in time of war. The unashamedly militaristic and jingoistic recruiting sermons preached by some bishops put clergy in the awkward position of the church seemingly being in favour of war but at the same time having its clergy exempt from service.

The British Expeditionary Force in 1914 was accompanied by 65 chaplains of various denominations under the leadership of Dr D J M Simms, who was the Senior Chaplain and a Presbyterian. A Church of England chaplain was attached to each field ambulance, together with oversight of 4 battalions. Chaplains of other denominations were also divided amongst the ambulances. However, no provision had been made for their attachment, rations, accommodation or transport. Many chaplains' first job was to find their unit and accommodate themselves as best they could. As the war progressed, the administration of the Chaplains' Department became more extensive, with the creation of divisional chaplains with responsibility for allocating chaplains to ambulances, hospitals or fighting units.

At first chaplains were associated with two major functions; providing recreational facilities and burying the dead. Many found this limiting, although the recreational mantle led to the setting up of Talbot House, and the work of the chaplains in keeping records of burial sites was to be of inestimable value to the Imperial War Graves Commission. The work of the chaplains, particularly the Church of England chaplains, was hindered in the first stages of the war by instructions not to go into the front line. It was felt that they would be in the way and become a nuisance to troops and manoeuvres. This led in post-war years to some unfavourable comparisons with the Roman Catholic priests who were unhindered by such orders. However, by early 1916, largely due to the pressure from chaplains themselves and a growing realisation of the army commanders that they could use the chaplains to maintain morale, these restricting orders had been largely removed and chaplains had more freedom to minister to troops under fire. Chaplains such as the Revd Geoffrey Studdert Kennedy and the Revd Neville Talbot had much to do with this change, as they were vociferous in their advocacy of the value of front line work.

The chaplain in the battlefields of the Great War then had a large number of opportunities to take and difficulties to overcome. Roger Lloyd, a Church of England historian, has said of the chaplain's situation, "He could indeed become necessary, but he must create that necessity himself."[4] Different priests sought out their usefulness in different ways, some in providing recreation and spiritual and physical sustenance away from the line, some caring for the needs of the wounded and dying and some sharing in the soldiers' lives in action in the trenches.

There has been continuing debate amongst historians about the efficacy and role of the Anglican chaplains in the war. Stephen Louden[5] in his examination of the army chaplains' role accuses them of being used by the army commanders to boost military morale and also that chaplains were more concerned with the social and material welfare of the troops than with their spiritual welfare. Alan Wilkinson[6] described the paradoxes surrounding the concept of military chaplaincy. Many of these become apparent when examining the dilemmas faced by the chaplains in the First World War.

Was what the Revd Neville Talbot called 'Holy Grocery', the attempts of chaplains to follow a wide brief in attempting to provide for the troops' physical and social welfare as well as their spiritual condition, a distraction from their real work? Or was it an essential part of witnessing to God's love in the awful conditions of war? Was the role of the chaplain in battle to be encouraging a limited number of men by accompanying them into action? Was it to minister to the needs of a greater number of men, both physical and spiritual, further back at aid posts? Where did their duty lie?

If we are to gain a clear picture of the nature and success of the work of the chaplains in the war then it is necessary to use their own accounts and those of their contemporaries to look at the ways that they overcame the tensions and ambiguities of their role. This book will look at the different aspects of the experiences of chaplains in the front line, at bases, in hospitals and battle and their roles in ministering physically and spiritually to the men in their care. Their accounts show a wide variety in the way that chaplains responded and adapted to the changing conditions of war. Some were exceptional, some were ordinary, but it is probable that they were often overwhelmed with the enormity of their task but concentrated above all in bringing the reality of God into the lives of the soldiers engaged in total war.

Notes

1. J.G. Smyth, *In this Sign Conquer*, p. 203.
2. Michael Snape, *God and the British Soldier*, p. 90.
3. Michael Snape, *Chaplains Under Fire*, p. 224.
4. Roger Lloyd, *The Church of England*, p. 215.
5. Stephen Louden, *Chaplains in Conflict*, pp. 43-67.
6. Alan Wilkinson, 'The Paradox of the Military Chaplain', *Theology*, 1984, p. 249.

Chapter 1

Recruitment and Deployment

War in 1914 came as the Anglican Church was struggling with internal conflicts arising from the growth of the Anglo-Catholic movement, the problems posed by modern biblical criticism, and the rise of secularism. There was a shortage of ordinands as compared to the rising population, particularly in towns and cities. Priests in the Anglican Church were required to have a degree, a familiarity with Greek and Latin and a working knowledge of Scripture and Theology. There was no absolute requirement to attend a theological college. Roger Lloyd, in his history of the Church of England, has calculated that in 1907 half the men ordained had not been to theological college.[1] This perhaps was just as well as the demand for places for theological training outstripped demand. The college of The Community of the Resurrection at Mirfield and the Society of the Sacred Mission at Kelham made strenuous efforts to rectify the situation, giving candidates a lengthy and rigorous training. These institutions were, however, held in suspicion by many for their Anglo – Catholic leanings. Some ordinands who were later to become chaplains, like Phillip 'Tubby' Clayton and William Drury, after taking degrees at Oxford, spent a year being trained in a small group by The Revd B K Cunningham at the Bishop of Winchester's Hostel at Farnham. The Revd Harry Blackburne, a regular army chaplain since 1903, spent some months after his degree at Cambridge at the home of The Revd J B Seaton of Leeds, attending lectures at Leeds Clergy School and being prepared for the Deacon's exam.

The curate or vicar who had been employed in a big town parish, e.g. St Mary's Portsea, would have been used to spending a large percentage of his time with boys and men in the many 'clubs' that were the Anglican churches answer to the decline of attendance of young men at church. He would also have been required to visit effectively and thoroughly all the people in the parish regardless of whether they attended church. Both these aspects of parish life were, in some ways, to prepare the Anglican town clergyman for his role in the trenches. From the parish of Portsea nine curates were to go to the front. Three were to be awarded the MC.

The outbreak of war and the rush of all types of civilians to the cause required some rapid decision-making by the hierarchy of the church and by individual clergy. The bishops and archbishops reacted with shock and horror. Bishop Gore of Oxford describing his feelings on war, "It cometh of the evil one."[2] The Archbishop of York, Cosmo Gordon Lang said "I hate war … it is the bankruptcy of Christian Principle",[3] but nevertheless most declared it a righteous war and put the support of the church behind it. Archbishop Cosmo Gordon Lang struggled with the problem on retreat in September 1914. "I was driven to the conclusion, right or wrong, that the war was righteous, that we were bound in honour to enter it, that the church could not rightly oppose it."[4] The question of whether the clergy should be allowed or encouraged to enlist as combatants soon arose. The Archbishop wrote unequivocally to the Diocesan bishops advising them that "The position of an active combatant in our army is incompatible with one who has sought and received holy orders."[5] Bishop Talbot of Winchester was of the opinion that "Those who minister about holy things and hold their lord's commission, must not have

The Revd J.M. Simms, Principal Chaplain, British
Expeditionary Force 1914-1918. (RAChD Archives)

blood on their hands however justly shed."[6] This left clergy and ordinands with some clear choices to stay put and minister to their home congregations, to give up their calling and enlist anyway, or to try and get accepted as an army chaplain. Most clergy were already asking themselves the big questions about the role of the church and religion in a major war. The Revd B K Cunningham asked himself "How could the church best present the gospel to such a world? ... Would the effect of war, and the suffering that it causes, drive people away from religion or was there a chance that out of the furnace would arise a purer and more devoted Christian church?"[7] As a leading figure in the lives of many clergy who had past through his hands at Farnham, he was asked frequently for advice of the best route for clergy and ordinands to take.

There was much public controversy about the way forward for ordinands, considerable pressure being felt by them to abandon their studies and join up as combatants. On the other hand, concerns were felt that in time when the spiritual needs of the population, both at home and in the army would be increasing, then it was shortsighted for future priests to withdraw from ordination. B K Cunningham, although aware of the need for the role of clergy in the war effort, seems to have erred on the side of sympathy of those who could not wait for ordination but who joined up, 362 in total at the outbreak of war. By Christmas 1914 over 30% of Mirfield ordinands had enlisted.[8] He argued that these men were not necessarily a loss to God's work in the trenches.

> To speak of the addition of 400 rifles as being of small worth compared with the loss of 400 priests is surely stupid, for any man who quietly witnesses to the faith that is in him and does what he can to be helpful to others is a great deal more than a 'rifle', indeed his opportunities might be envied by any chaplain![9]

On the question of already ordained men serving in parishes, he encouraged men who were able easily to enlist without leaving a parish in difficulties to do so:

If a man is a curate in a small parish from which he can be spared ... he surely has no right to continue there in these days. If he likes men and is ready to serve men in every conceivable form of service ... ought he not to apply for a chaplaincy? Otherwise he has to consider whether to enlist as a private in the RAMC is the best service he can render.[10]

On the other hand he felt keenly the dilemma of priests who could not be spared and were not given permission by their Bishops to join up. "These must expect to be misunderstood and they must just face up to it."[11] Archbishop Gordon Lang realised that "Not all, even the younger clergy, who were in charge of parishes could be spared ... I was indignant later when I discovered some of the chaplains resented the position of their brethren who held the fort at home, for I knew that for them this was by far the harder part."[12] An insight into the Archbishop of York's view is given by Canon Samuel Bickersteth, who spent a weekend at Bishopthorpe at the end of August.

The Archbishop was quite in favour of men trying to get to the front, but he lost patience with those who had gone and should have remained at their post at home, for example, Dick Sheppard who was in charge of Grosvenor Chapel and had just been appointed to St Martin in the Fields.

The Archbishop referred with approval to Neville Talbot who "Just happened to be free, having left his work at Balliol and not yet gone to India", but looked on the Bishop of London's announcement that he intended going with the London Rifle Brigade for six months as "a piece of rather dramatic playing to the gallery."[13]

The Revd Samuel Leighton Green was in this position for the first part of the war as his vicar had gone to France at the outbreak of war as a motorcyclist with the Red Cross and it was only on his return that Green was able to offer his services as an army chaplain. Similarly, the Revd Geoffrey Studdert Kennedy was delayed from joining the Chaplains' Department until December 1915 because of the difficulties of making adequate arrangements for his parish in Worcester.

Clergy reacted in various ways to the dilemma. Neville Talbot, son of Bishop Talbot wrote "I feel that a great deal of our long peace has been a false peace, oblivious to God and his righteousness. My thoughts turn to a chaplaincy to the troops."[14] The Revd F R Barry was ordained in June 1914 after a year as a fellow of Oriel College Oxford. He at first thought it his duty to stay at Oxford "to hold on and try and shepherd the remnant of the college in a stricken and depopulated Oxford",[15] but by September 1915, after his ordination as priest, he was commissioned as an army chaplain. The Revd William Drury was visited by his old university friend the Revd Phillip 'Tubby' Clayton at the end of August and they discussed the situation.

According to William Drury, Phillip Clayton had been a pacifist but had now quite changed his views. "He said that after the war there would be only two kinds of men, those who had been in it and those who had not". At the same time they discussed the propriety of joining up immediately when they had heard rumours that many of the regular chaplains were kept at home while certain picked men from our civilian clergy were being sent abroad as volunteers. William Drury consulted with the Bishop of Guildford. He says "I felt that perhaps I should perhaps go as a chaplain, but those whose opinion I could best trust seemed to think that I should carry on the ordinary duties at home and the doctor admitted that he would himself not pass me for service abroad."

The Right Revd A. Winnington-Ingram. (Bishop of London)

Despite these early reservations, by July, Drury had applied and been accepted by the Army Chaplains' Department.[16]

The situation was indeed uncertain in the first weeks of the war. Roger Lloyd points out that the situation was complicated by the fact that it was difficult to get accurate numbers of how many chaplains were wanted from the War Office and there was some uncertainty about whether clergy would be called up for service as chaplains. This did not stop many priests from applying immediately to be chaplains. According to Alan Wilkinson, 900 more than were required had volunteered by 1 September 1914. The Archbishop described the situation in December as chaotically unsolved. It was by no means easy to get accepted immediately. The Revd Edmund Kennedy, who was a territorial chaplain, had "at the earliest moment possible volunteered my services to the army"[17] but was told that he was not wanted at that time. A few days later he was called upon with 'alarming suddenness' and whisked away to join the Seventh Division which was embarking for France. Christopher Chavasse, son of the Bishop of Liverpool, whose telegram asking the Bishop's permission to join the Army Chaplains' Department had crossed with one from his father advising him to do so, was quickly accepted for service with the Fourth Army Corps and left for France on 20 August 1914.

Having applied to be a chaplain, the next hurdle to be got over was the personal interview with the Chaplain General, Bishop Taylor Smith. The Chaplain General had a bad reputation in the history of the Army Chaplains' Department's involvement in the First World War. He had been castigated as a rabid evangelical who did not like appointing Anglo-Catholic priests and was biased against their selection. He was also criticised for his non-intellectual missionary background. Stories abound about his method of interviewing. The Revd William Drury recounts his interview. "He was searching enough on some points. What did I find my chief difficulty? I mentioned that I did not find it easy to control boys, whereupon he remarked "he who cannot discipline others does not usually discipline himself." Drury was asked the apparently favourite question used by the Bishop, "What would you do if you found yourself in the presence

The Revd J. Taylor Smith, Chaplain-General 1901-25, and
the Revd A.C.E. Jarvis, Chaplain-General 1925–31. (RAChD Archives)

of a man who had but five minutes to live?" Drury mentioned praying with him but apparently the right answer should have been, according to the Bishop "I should hold up before him Christ crucified."[18] Drury goes on to relate how throughout the first part of the war the Bishop would not forego interviewing every candidate. He then recorded his opinions on a card file system that still exists in the Army Chaplains' Department archives. The Revd Leighton Green, who was accepted despite his clear Anglo – Catholic persuasion, had the dubious epithet of "a very mincing manner"[19] put on his card. In his biography of Taylor Smith, E L Langton has a different view of his interviewing methods. He regards the famous question about dealing with a man who had five minutes to live as a very serious and astute one. "It was clearly a question of a man deeply in earnest in seeking the spiritual efficiency in his department."[20] He does not consider that the question of churchmanship had much to do with selection. "The Chaplain General recognised that the men of the new army would require the type of chaplain who would understand their varied mentalities and spiritual outlooks."[21]

The Revd E C Crosse reflected how ill-equipped chaplains were to face the rigours of army camps and trench life. King's Regulations were sparse in their advice as they simply required chaplains to conduct parade and voluntary services and to perform burials. He bemoans the fact that in the early days the chaplain received no sort of preliminary training. "He went straight from his parish to his unit and was left almost entirely to gain his experience for himself. Even a month spent at some preliminary school of army training would have saved many needless errors."[22] He recalls a visit at his first camp at Bisley from a senior chaplain who spent most of the time grumbling about his pay. He considers that chaplains were sent to camps ignorant of army life and protocol. Some small questions which would not have taken long to sort out in the right circumstances loomed large in Crosse's mind, "should the chaplain wear a belt? should a chaplain be saluted? should he wear a moustache? All these seem in a way silly little points, but may serve as an illustration of how lost one felt in one's new surroundings with no one whatever to whom to apply for guidance."[23] Once a chaplain was posted abroad he was issued with a communion set and after 1915, he was allowed 350 field service books. The army agreed to supply each chaplain with a horse when his duties required one. This was changed in 1917 when the horse casualties necessitated the replacement of the chaplain's horse with a bicycle.

Bishop Taylor Smith had, before the war, put forward a scheme setting out the place of a chaplain in time of war but this had not been accepted or implemented. The result was the chaotic deployment of chaplains in the first months of the war. At the beginning of the war the Chaplain's Department had 117 chaplains, 65 of whom went to France immediately. These were soon supplemented by territorial chaplains who were mobilised, or by volunteers. There seemed to be no rhyme or reason to selection. Some volunteers had to wait, others were mobilised within a few days. The Revd Edmund Kennedy was sent to join the Seventh Division which he describes as the "First division to march out of an English camp fully equipped."[24] There were two Anglican chaplains, a Roman Catholic and a Presbyterian attached to the division and Kennedy himself was attached to the 23rd Field Ambulance serving the 20th Brigade. He seems to have been lucky to be part of a well-organised complete division. In many cases little provision was made for transporting, feeding or billeting of chaplains. According to the Revd Barry, "The army seems to have little idea of what to do with them."[25] As many of them were attached to field ambulances they were not seen at the firing line and were encouraged by senior officers to keep behind the lines. It is from this confusion that the idea that Anglican chaplains were in some way cowardly gained ground. When the Revd E C Crosse arrived with his division in France in 1915 he was told his main job was to "Visit his battalion regularly as they come out of the line — my senior chaplain told me that it was absolutely forbidden for me to go into the line at all."[26] The Assistant Chaplain General, 4th Army, H J Southwell, gave the following order as late as June 1916:

> Chaplains should under no circumstances advance with their regiments or brigade … This order is to be strictly obeyed and S. C. F.'s C/E . are responsible for making it known to all the C of E chaplains in the division[27]

We shall see the orders concerning the position of chaplains in battle were changed early in 1916 giving much greater freedom of movement, but much of the damage that resulted in army chaplains receiving a bad press had already been done, as a direct result of the confusion surrounding their role early in the war.

Meanwhile on other fronts the organisation and deployment of chaplains progressed along different lines. The Principal Chaplain in the Middle East was the Revd A W Horden. He was in charge of chaplains of all denominations and responsible for their care and deployment. The landings in Gallipoli in 1915 put huge strain on a chaplains' force that was only sporadically being reinforced from England. In his War Diaries, the Revd Horden is constantly bemoaning the lack of chaplains and trying to keep up with demands for chaplains on the peninsula, and on hospital ships, at hospitals and base camps back in Egypt. It would seem that, in contrast to the slightly ambivalent attitude to chaplains shown by the army on the Western Front, chaplains were being urgently requested. On 3 June he writes of a request made "Could I possibly send chaplains for troopships ordered to Gallipoli at once to take off wounded. By taking away chaplains employed at base camps, I managed."[28] In December 1915 Horden also took over responsibility for the Macedonian front in Salonika.

The Expeditionary Force in Mesopotamia had been sent to protect British oil interests in the Persian Gulf. For the first two years of the war all chaplains sent to this theatre were from the Indian church and in 1915, when the Bishop of Lahore arrived at the Macedonia Front, there were only 4 chaplains there. "The Revd Ormond Birchat Nasariyeh on the Euphrates, the Revds Bridge and Tibbs at Basra and the Revd Harold Spooner on the Tigris."[29] Eventually the War Office took responsibility for the chaplains in Mesopotamia and appointed a principal chaplain and 5 senior chaplains, but during the first part of the war the very small force of army chaplains had to cope.

The Army Chaplains' Department in 1914 and 1915 had to deal with multiple problems of recruitment, deployment and questions about its role in modern warfare. Its organisation and administrative skills were embryonic and it had great deal to do to become an efficient part of the army. However, in the same way that fighting units were to learn and adapt to changing conditions of trench warfare, so would the Department.

Notes

1.   Roger Lloyd, *The Church of England*, p. 150.
2.   Alan Wilkinson, *The Church of England and the First World War*, p. 16.
3.   Ibid.
4.   J. G. Lockhart, *Cosmo Gordon Lang*, p. 246.
5.   J. R. Moorman, *B.K. Cunningham*, p. 72.
6.   Ibid, p. 71.
7.   Ibid, p. 76.
8.   Wilkinson, op. cit., p. 37.
9.   Moorman, op. cit., p. 73.
10. Ibid.
11. Ibid.
12. Lockhart, op.cit, p. 247.
13. John Bickersteth, *The Bickersteth Diaries*, p. 3.
14. F. H. Brabant, *Neville Stuart Talbot*, quoted by Wilkinson, op. cit., p. 29.
15. F. R. Barry, *Period of my Life*, p. 51.
16. William Drury, *Camp Follower*, p. 13.
17. E. J. Kennedy, *With the Immortal Seventh Division*, p. 7
18. Drury, op. cit., p. 14.
19. S. J. Maclaren, *Somewhere in Flanders. Letters of a Norfolk Padre in the Great War*, p. 13.
20. E. L. Langston, *Bishop Taylor Smith*, p. 129.
21. Langton, op. cit., p. 127.
22. E.C. Crosse Papers, IWM (80/22/1), p. 28.
23. Ibid, p. 29.
24. Kennedy, op. cit., p. 10
25. Barry, op. cit., p. 60.
26. Crosse, op. cit. p. 52.
27. Richard Schweitzer, *The Cross and the Trenches*, p. 169.
28. A. W. Horden, War Diary of the Principal Chaplain (WO/95/2023)
29. Ibid.
30. Bishop of Lahore, 'The R. A. Ch. D. in Mesopotamia', *Royal Army Chaplains' Department Quarterly Journal* Vol 2 No 7 (July 1923), pp.266-268.

Chapter 2

Making a role. Chaplains 1914–16

Amid the confusion of the recruitment and early deployment of temporary chaplains, the regular chaplains were embarked for France and involved in the retreat from Mons and the Battle of the Marne. The Fifth Division under the command of Sir H L Smith-Dorrien had arrived in France on 22 August 1914. The Revd Douglas Winnifrith, Anglican chaplain attached to the 14th Field Ambulance was very aware that the action had started and was keen to get on with things. "We knew that the field ambulance would be needed and were all anxious to do our bit."[1] It was at Dour on 24 August that the 14th Ambulance caught up with the retiring 14th Infantry Brigade. From then on they were involved day by day with the retreat. On the 25th they passed through the Forêt de Normal to Le Cateau.

At Honnechy the role of the ambulance was to support the fighting that was going on at Le Cateau. The attitude of some officers to chaplains at this stage of the war is shown by a comment made to Winnifrith by an officer – "Good morning Padre, this is no place for you or the hospital; it will be a warm spot soon". Winnifrith assured the officer that "the padre and doctors were not going to desert them and would be close at hand if needed."[2] Winnifrith did indeed find himself fully occupied assisting in a farm house which had been turned into a temporary ward, holding limbs while the doctor bandaged them and giving "a word of prayer here and there".[3] As the retreat continued Winnifrith was exercised with the dilemma of leaving the wounded in the wake of the retreat. "I deeply regretted that permission could not be given me to remain behind to bury our comrades who had fallen."[4] Two chaplains were in fact taken prisoner during the retreat, the Revd J T Hales and the Revd B J O'Rourke, who were not released until 10 months later. He also commented on the lack of time to provide church services, especially on Sundays, but he was of the opinion that the lack of public worship was more than made up for by private prayers and thoughts.

On 10 September an advanced dressing station was established at Passey and Winnifrith was instructed to take the wounded to a nearby village to be evacuated. On 10 September Winnifrith and the Revd O S Watkins, his Methodist colleague, set out to find the bodies of the dead. The war diary of the 14th Ambulance mentions that on 10 September, 3 officers and 38 other ranks were found dead by the chaplains and buried.

> We decided to go over the battlefield in different directions to bury any dead we could find, irrespective of religious denomination. Whenever we found a fallen comrade we bore his body to the corner of the field to secure it … and there dug a shallow grave.[5]

This was the first time that the chaplains had been able to fulfil their duties of burial as up to then the army had been in swift retreat. The two chaplains marked the graves with a rough cross and kept a record of the names of the men that they buried and the location of their graves. This role of record keeping of graves was to become vital to the latter work of the Commonwealth Graves Commission.

The Revd D. Winnifrith, 14th Infantry Brigade. (Private collection)

The Revd H Blackburne, a regular chaplain who had also served in the Boer War as a soldier, and was later to become Assistant Chaplain General of the First Army, has also left a record of his experiences in the early days of the war. After taking part in the retreat from Mons, he was at Vendresse, housed in the cellar of a chapel. He was able to have services there. "Parties of men keep coming in for short services before going to take their place in the trenches on the hill." He continues "every evening before the wounded are evacuated we have a few prayers and sing a hymn".[6] He also found burying the dead to be a large part of his job. "I bury the dead each night in the village cemetery. Sometimes I have to dig the graves myself".[7] Like Winnifrith he kept a careful record of all his funerals, with map references. He then moved on to Ypres, and describes a day in which he had four "wonderful services".[8]

The memoirs of regular Army chaplains like Winnifrith, Watkins and Blackburne show how, from the opening stages of the war, chaplains were close to the troops they served and contributed in a multiplicity of ways to the units they were attached to. However, it must be remembered that they were regulars, well used to dealing with their men. Alan Wilkinson has pointed out that in some cases to the ordinary soldier the chaplain seemed socially a class apart and quotes Harold Wooley, later to be a chaplain in the Second World War, recounting that it was more than a month after landing in France in November 1914 before he saw a chaplain.[9]

Meanwhile, many chaplains arriving in France had a more frustrating time. The mobilisation plans did not include plans for transporting, accommodating, paying or even feeding chaplains. Even as late as 1916 the Revd Drury after having being posted temporarily to a different field ambulance experienced embarrassment in having to share the rations of his fellow officers when obviously no provision had been made for him. The Revd F R Barry described the problem.

When the padres first went out with the BEF the army had little idea of what to do with them. In battle they were left behind at the base and were not allowed to go up

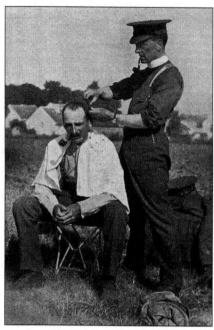

The Revd D. Winnnifrith acting as barber for his Methodist
colleague, The Revd O. S. Watkins. (Private collection)

to the fighting front ... A colonel would say "No work for you to do today, padre."
Meaning by that no corpses for burial.[10]

As a result of this early prohibition of going into the front line much of the chaplain's
work was with the men at camps and billet, performing a more social role. Many
chaplains threw themselves in to the task of manning church army recreation huts and
maintaining the constant flow of essentials of every kind. Barry goes on to describe their
main occupations.

The chaplain's job was take church parades, on such rare occasions as these were
practicable, to run entertainments, to help in censoring letters and in general to act
as welfare officers. But was that what they had been ordained to do?[11]

Two of the most famous and revered chaplains that the Great War produced
based their ministries on providing material and physical relief for the troops as well as
ministering to their spiritual needs – the Revd Studdert Kennedy with his cigarettes,
'Woodbine Willy', and the Revd 'Tubby' Clayton with his centre providing rest and
recreation for the troops at Talbot House.

A chaplain who arrived in France comparatively early in the war, just in time for the
First Battle of Ypres was the Revd E Kennedy. He was appointed to the 7th Division and
came over to France with them, landing at Zeebrugge and gives a stirring account of their
march across Belgium. His role appears to have been billeting officer and he seems to have
provided this service with great gusto. Having arrived at Ypres, the division was rapidly
thrown into the fighting and Kennedy was kept busy with the field ambulance. His unit

The Revd E.J. Kennedy, Chaplain 7th Division. (Private collection)

then moved to a line of trenches in the vicinity of Zanvoorde, at one point ending up being posted in front of the firing line.

"Disturbing sniping took place at intervals throughout the night which rendered the bivouac unpleasant in the extreme."[12] At the height of the battle Kennedy was asked by the commanding officer to get through to Ypres. He was to warn the Major of the serious condition of affairs at Zanworde and stop the transport that was about to come out. Kennedy grabbed his horse and embarked on what he described as

> The ride of my life. Shells were bursting in every direction … I could only place myself in God's hands … I repeated those comforting words from Isaiah xxvi 'Thou will keep him in perfect peace whose mind is stayed on thee, because he trusteth in thee.'[13]

A few days after this experience he had to bury Prince Maurice of Battenburg. Kennedy was injured a few weeks later by his horse falling heavily on him and went home on a hospital ship, to return and continue his wartime ministry mainly in camps and behind the lines, but the early experiences of this chaplain not in his first flush of youth show that all was not disorganisation and chaos in an army chaplain's life.

Another elderly chaplain who became famous for breaking through red tape and military restrictions was Canon Frederick Scott. He was one of the chaplains accompanying the Canadian forces to England in preparation for their role on the Western Front. On hearing that he was not to go to France but rather he was to be posted in England to the No. 2 General Hospital, he 'decided' that he did not know where this hospital was and actually stowed away on a transport ship to France in order to 'find' his placement. On discovery in France, he managed to attach himself to a brigade and did not get sent back. He went on to become the most decorated and loved of the Canadian chaplains, serving on all sectors of the Western Front.

The pressure had been rising within the Anglican clergy for restrictions on their movements to be lifted. As early as October 1914 the Revd Neville Talbot was writing to his senior chaplain,

> There is much scope and work to be done with a unit as a whole and with fighting troops. One can get to know them, see them in trenches, help them about daily prayers, have services with them when they are in the billets ... and be available for help in other ways.[14]

A letter written by the Revd Guy Rogers in December 1915 shows that not all chaplains obeyed these orders. "I'm sure you have guessed that my work often takes me into the trenches, it is a tradition, it is expected and what one's influence largely depends, going in and out amongst the men where they are"[15]. Bishop Gwynne and other bishops, as well as *The Guardian* newspaper, had been agitating for change. Alan Wilkinson, in his study of the Anglican church in the First World War, is convinced that Neville Talbot's opinions as expressed to the army authorities had a great deal of effect on the decision to change the order.

By the beginning of 1916 the situation had changed. The Revd Barry described that "The Chaplains were allowed to move more freely everywhere and when the units went up we went with them. ... We would give Holy Communion in the dug outs, minister to the wounded and dying, share, so far as we might in what the troops endured."[16] The Revd E C Crosse recounted how the priorities of chaplains underwent change as the war progressed. "The thoughtful padre was compelled ... to examine without prejudice the original idea that that his work lies primarily with the sick or wounded." He described how it had been assumed that men would have more use for the ministrations of the clergy on their deathbed. He explained how "The experience of war ran counter to this argument."[17] This was because at the front those who had a 'blighty wound' did not consider themselves in need of sympathy and often were moved on swiftly out of the chaplains' care. Instead he thought that the chaplain should be concentrating on those who were "accessible and in need of all the encouragement they could get, namely the unwounded duty man."[18] He had strong opinions on the place of the chaplain in the trenches. "Gradually it became obvious that the right place for the padre was at the H.Q. of one of his two battalions, and that the place where he could be most useful was in the line itself."[19] The Revd Guy Rogers, who found himself looking after 4 battalions of Guards, however, realised the enormity of the seemingly never ending role. "My task of looking after the brigade is beyond my powers. This minority of the Scots is neglected. I have so often had to let them slide"[20]

The organisation of the work of the Anglican army chaplains was enhanced enormously by the appointment of the Bishop of Khartoum, the Revd Harry Gwynne as Deputy Chaplain General in July 1915 with responsibility for Anglican chaplains in France. Harry Blackburne's comment was "It looks as if the Chaplains Department is at last to be properly organised."[21] There had been criticisms of the way the Army Chaplains' Department was organised, with grumbles about the discrimination against the more catholic clergy by Bishop Taylor Smith. The church press and the national press were pressing for closer care and supervision for Anglican chaplains at the Front. Bishop Gwynne turned his attention to supporting and organising the chaplains in France to good effect. He gave support to the more catholic Anglican clergy and "was loved and trusted by all alike."[22]

At the same time Blackburne was promoted to Senior Chaplain of the First Division, followed early in 1916 by a move to be Senior Chaplain, First Army. Later this job description was changed to Assistant Chaplain General. His work was now concerned more with the organisation of the Chaplains' Department and the welfare and deployment of the chaplains beneath him. One of his first schemes was one whereby each chaplain in the First Army in charge of a casualty clearing station would have several units to look after as well as a hospital. "In this way we ought to link up with most units in the whole army area."[23] This was to be typical of the way the Army Chaplains' Department was to increasingly think, leading to a better relationship between Anglican clergy and their troops.

By the beginning of 1916, therefore, the Army Chaplains' Department had overcome several ideological and practical problems relating to its deployment and was present at battalion level as well as being attached to base hospital, headquarters and ambulances. As Blackburne said on 17 Feb 1916 "Now that the establishments of chaplains have doubled, it is altogether inexcusable if either officers or men are ignorant of who is the padre."[24] The Revd Julian Bickersteth, arriving in the Somme area in February 1916, wrote of a divisional chaplains' meeting called by the Senior Chaplain in which he met the other chaplains and the dispositions of the chaplains were discussed. "The Senior Chaplain went through our areas with us and we settled up everything so that there was no overlapping and that every unit, however small, in the division got the opportunity of ministrations of some chaplain or another."[25] The Revd Crosse recalled how changes made in the disposition of chaplains by their Senior Chaplains worked in practice.

In General this worked out as follows. Of the three field ambulances in a division one would usually be detailed as the main dressing station some three or five miles behind the line the other two being attached to attacking brigades and each being subdivided into a dressing station and an advanced dressing station. To each field ambulance one chaplain, at least, would be assigned … permission would probably be given to the remaining chaplains to accompany their men if they wished – nor was there often a lack of volunteers for this job.[26]

In his wartime papers, now housed at the Royal Army Chaplains' Department museum in Amport House, Andover, Blackburne has left a wealth of detail on the organisation and priorities of the First Army Chaplains. The Senior Chaplain of a division must have weekly meetings of his chaplains. "It is up to the senior chaplain to make it attractive and refreshing, that chaplains will look forward to it all week,"[27] he advised. They were to begin with Holy Communion. The business of the meetings were to discuss "plans and principles" for the present and future work and then to have a study circle and/or sermon planning. After what seems like a rigorous morning the afternoon was to be devoted to a more relaxing atmosphere "friendly talk and ragging."[28] Blackburne was evidently concerned with the maintenance of morale amongst his chaplains. He exhorts the Senior Chaplain to take into account the loneliness experienced by many chaplains.

The Revd G A Weston was the senior chaplain to the 18th Division in the months leading up to and during the Battle of the Somme in July 1916. In his divisional war diaries he gives an illuminating account of the role of the Senior Chaplain. He called a meeting of his chaplains from the 53rd, 54th and 55th Infantry Brigades on 31 August. The meeting opened with a devotional service and Weston then talked to the chaplains about the National Mission for Hope and Repentance and its relevance to the chaplains and troops in the trenches. On a more practical note the business continued with the amendments to the GRO's information about recent burials and "the disposition of the deceased."[29] During the height of the Battle of the Somme it was important that the chaplains continued their vital work of making accurate notes on burial sites. Another meeting was held on 14 September. At his time the division were preparing for the assault on Thiepval Village and Schwaben Redoubt and part of the business of the meeting was to discuss the situation of the Divisional Chaplains in the coming battle. Two of the chaplains attached to the 55th Brigade were detached from their regiments and attached to a dressing station at Clairfaye Farm, whereas the chaplains of the 54th and 53rd Brigades were notified that they were to be responsible for all areas east of Heudaville and were to be based at Aveuly Post and Wood Post. The diaries showed clearly the increasing care taken to ensure that chaplains were in the right place and attention was paid to the liaison of chaplains of different denominations. However this thought given to the role of chaplains was not consistent throughout the different armies. An order was given by the Fourth Army just before the Battle of the Somme expressing what Crosse calls 'The Old Heresy', that the chaplains' work was with the wounded and forbidding them to go up to the line. Crosse says that this order brought so many protests from the chaplains that it was altered, allowing more latitude to a limited number of chaplains. He goes on "as a consequence several chaplains did in fact accompany their battalions into battle and we never heard later of any order restricting their activities."[30] In contrast the Fifth Army order of battle, issued by General Gough was to the effect that chaplains should be allowed to go where they liked. This practice gradually became adopted by all armies.

The chaplains in Gallipoli were facing some of the same difficulties, the continuous flow of casualties from Gallipoli resulted in a strain on the chaplains based in the Middle East, who were understaffed and suffering from illness at an alarming rate. The Principal Chaplain, the Revd Horden visited the Gallipoli GHQ on 21 June 1915 where he formed an impression of the conditions on the peninsula. "The difficulties are very great as no part of the peninsula is free from shell fire." He returned in November and commented, "the men who have been for any length of time in the peninsula seem to suffer from the strain, no place being free from shell fire. I propose to change their stations as the opportunity occurs."[31] Horden's problems were added to when he became additionally responsible for the chaplains on the Salonika Front in December 1915. He visited Salonika on the 29th and found "six hospitals and casualty clearing stations without chaplains." He visited all the hospitals and reorganised the disposition of chaplains.[32]

By the beginning of 1916, many of the initial difficulties experienced by Chaplains in the early days of the war were being resolved. The generals had a good opinion of the work of the chaplains and their effects on morale. When Archbishop Davidson went to France in May 1916 he pressed Haig for criticisms of the chaplains "but I could not elicit anything except laudation."[33] As we will see later this rapport between the Chaplains' Department and High Command was to lead to post-war criticism of the chaplains' role, but at the time it made the organisation of the department more effective. The organisation of the department had improved considerably and there was a much greater chance of a chaplain being in the right place at the right time. There was still a considerable tension in the Anglican army chaplains about the relative importance and prioritisation of entertainment and what Neville Talbot called 'Holy Grocery' as opposed to spiritual work with the troops. The Revd Geoffrey Gordon felt this dilemma keenly. "Those of us chaplains who feel ourselves pressed by our dilemma are occupying much of our time with things that the soldier would describe as non religious, but on every opportunity we are preaching constantly and insistently the all inclusiveness of Christianity."[34] However, the Chaplains' Department now had a better infrastructure of support for its chaplains and many individual chaplains were beginning to feel that their efforts were appreciated. As Harry Blackburne put it "There's a job all right for a padre out here."[35]

Notes

1. D. Winnifrith, *The Church in the Fighting Line*, p. 19.
2. Ibid, p. 35.
3. Ibid, p. 37.
4. Ibid, p. 44.
5. Ibid, p.70.
6. H. Blackburne, *This Also Happened On The Western Front*, p. 16.
7. Ibid.
8. Ibid, p. 25.
9. Alan Wilkinson, *The Church of England and the First World War*, p. 131.
10. F.R. Barry, *Period of my Life*, p. 60.
11. Ibid.
12. E.J. Kennedy, *With the Immortal 7th Division*, p. 43.
13. Ibid, p. 55.
14. Wilkinson, op. cit., p. 130.
15. Guy Rogers Papers, IWM (77/10/11).
16. Barry, op.cit.
17. E.C. Crosse Papers, IWM (80/22/1), p. 53.
18. Ibid.
19. Ibid, pp. 54-55.
20. Rogers, op. cit.
21. Blackburne, op. cit., p. 56.
22. Roger Lloyd, *The Church of England*, p. 216.
23. Blackburne, op. cit., p 80.
24. RACh Archives.
25. John Bickersteth (ed), *The Bickersteth Diaries*, p. 78.
26. Crosse, op. cit., p. 69.
27. RAchD archives.
28. Ibid.
29. G.A.Weston, War Diary of the Senior Chaplain to the 18th Division (WO 95/2023)
30. Crosse,op. cit.,p. 69
31. Revd A W Horden, War Diary of the Principal Chaplain (WO/95/2023)
32. Horden, Ibid
33. Wilkinson, op. cit.,p 131
34. The Revd G.Gordon, Papers from Picardy,p.112
35. H. Blackburne, *This also Happened on the Western Front*, p.19

Chapter 3

Chaplains in Action

As we have seen in the previous chapter the organisation of the Chaplains' Department had improved considerably by the beginning of 1916, and the role of the chaplains in action was to be tested by the major event of that year – the offensive in the Somme area starting in July. The role that chaplains played in this battle has been well documented by the chaplains themselves and also commented on by generals and officers involved in the offensive.

The Revd Julian Bickersteth arrived on the Somme from school teaching in Australia in February 1916. He was the son of the Revd Samuel Bickersteth of Leeds and belonged to a large Christian family. Two of his brothers were serving in the same area as him during 1916. Although he was pleased with the response of the troops to the celebration of Easter in the trenches, he was soon caught up with practical preparations for the coming offensive and comments in June "We are training very hard, so hard that that Sunday is no longer a day of rest. No Church Parades were possible yesterday at all."[1] By 4 June he was very near the front line and conducting services in an underground chapel. He was holding communion services every morning and as the preliminary bombardment increased so did his congregations. "The services on 25th June in barns or in the open air were non-stop from 7 am."[2] Bickersteth wrote home on 26 June, reporting that his place in the coming battle was to be at an advanced dressing station. "How happy I am to be in being able to be in this great effort."[3]

The 56th Division was involved in the diversionary attack on Gommecourt, together with the 46th Division. Five days after the first day offensive, in which his brother Morris was killed, he wrote home with his thoughts and an account of his part in the battle. Together with two other Church of England chaplains, the Revd Crisford, and the Revd Palmer, Bickersteth dealt with returning casualties from the attack on 1 July at an advanced dressing station. "They began to arrive in ever increasing numbers ... I was being given different jobs to do by the doctor in charge, first to get away the walking wounded, then to superintend the loading of cars and then to see that the worst cases had 'Oxo' or hot tea to prevent collapse."[4] In the evening there were reports of wounded lying out in the trenches who could not be brought down from the front line. Three parties of the least-tired stretcher-bearers were formed and each put under the charge of one chaplain. They went into three different sections of the trenches to bring in as many wounded as possible. The Revd Crisford was wounded in this operation. The next day they began identifying and burying the dead. Bickersteth organised the digging of a large trench. At midday an armistice was announced to bring in the wounded and the Revd Palmer got as far as the German lines in his efforts to make sure there were no wounded left lying out in No Mans' Land. Taking turns with Palmer, Bickersteth spent the evening burying the dead. The Revd Palmer was awarded the MC in recognition of his work in bringing in the wounded.

The Revd William Drury was also involved in this two-pronged diversionary attack on Gommecourt. He was initially attached, in the Senior Chaplain's deployment plans, to the 2/1 Ambulance at Mondicourt. His first task was to look after the shellshock cases, but it was soon his turn to get nearer the action as he was sent forward to replace the Revd Crisford who had been wounded bringing in casualties. He recounts how the advanced dressing station was in an elephant bunker. On the first night of his new posting he was required to lead a party to find three bodies that had lain in the support trench since 1 July. On Sunday 9 July he found a half-ruined barn where he held a service of Holy Communion at which everyone wore their steel helmets as the service was carried out under machine gun fire. After a few weeks further back at St Riquier and at the Citadel Camp he was sent to a small dressing station called Dublin Post. Here he supported the work of the doctors and stretcher-bearers dealing with the wounded of the 56th Division fighting at Leuze Wood on 5 and 6 September. He was shocked at the difference between an advanced dressing station and the main dressing stations at the rear – "one saw the unalleviated horror of wounds."[5]

Drury was not the only chaplain to arrive at battlefields on the Somme untried and unaware what was in store. The Revd F R Barry was attached to the 5th Dorsets and was moved with them from Egypt to the Somme where they were involved in the attack on Moquet Farm in which he recounts that half his brigade was annihilated.

> I had never seen a dead man before, much less bloody bits and pieces of men, and as near as nothing I turned and ran. They thought I was brave, but in fact I was too innocent fully to appreciate the dangers.[6]

A chaplain assisting in bringing in the wounded, La Boiselle, Amiens Road July 1916. (IWM Q721)

The inwardly quaking Barry must have made a good impression, however as he was shortly to be made Senior Chaplain of the 20th Division.

The attitude towards the presence of chaplains near the front line was changing and as the Battle of the Somme wore on, the chaplains showed themselves able to be of use in the battle situation. This acceptance by officers, men and the chaplains themselves that their place was with the men in time of battle was encouraged by the words and actions of the Revd G Studdert Kennedy – 'Woodbine Willy'. Just after the attack on Gommecout, Drury bumped into him at Fonquuevillers and accompanied Studdert Kennedy on some trips to forward posts. He was impressed by his belief that a padre should make a point of seeking out the dangerous spots in order to counteract the idea that being a chaplain was a soft job. Later Drury was to encounter Studdert Kennedy again at the Chaplains' School of Instruction at St Omer. He remembers "At St Omer he urged us chaplains to seek the most dangerous positions as our presence was the best expression we could give of our message to the troops."[7]

The war diaries of The Revd G A Weston available from August to November 1916 give a very clear picture of the role of the divisional and brigade chaplains at the time of the battle of the Somme. By 25 August the division was on the move to a new DHQ at Rollecourt. Weston took the opportunity to send a circular to all his divisional chaplains informing them of the disposition of troops in this new area and suggesting a plan of cooperation to provide services for groups stationed there. Evidently the chaplains had developed the administrative structure to accommodate frequent movements of troops without it having a detrimental effect on the spiritual and pastoral care of the troops, although he admits to difficulties the following Sunday, 27 August in arranging services "Few services today because of training."[8] The fine weather of Sunday, 3 September meant open air church parades. The war diary of the 7th Bedfordshires reports an open air service been held in a field behind Tiloye Church.[9] When Weston rode over a few days later to

A burial on the battlefield. (Author's collection)

visit the 55th Brigade, the chaplain attached to the brigade, the Revd V C Boddington was able to report to his senior chaplain "A considerable number of communicants from the 7th Buffs and 7th Royal West Kents last Sunday."[10]

From 9-11 September the DHQ was being moved from Doullens to Acheux and by the 29th it was at Heudville as the division were preparing for the assault on Thiepval and Schwaben Redoubt. In preparation for the attack, the chaplains of the 55th Brigade, the Revds Stopford and Bodington were detached from their regiments and attached to the dressing station at Clairfaye Farm in readiness for the expected battle. Other chaplains from the 54th and 53rd Brigades were put in position with dressing stations at Aveluy and Wood Posts. In his diary entry for 24 September, Weston reported on the attack that resulted in the capture of Thiepval. He had ridden that day to visit the chaplains working at the advanced dressing stations at Aveluy Post and Black Horse Ridge. He gives some detail about the deployment of his chaplains at various aid posts and at Clairfaye Farm. The Revds Boddington and Stopford had been "working two days and a night" attending to the spiritual and physical needs of the wounded. The Revd R Wheller, who was with the 12th Middlesex, had received a gunshot wound to the arm but was continuing to work. The Chaplains had been performing battlefield funerals and "still had much work to do at the dressing stations."[11]

On the 2nd, the 54th and 53rd Brigades were relieved by the 55th Brigade. This gave the chaplains who had been at Clairfaye Farm the opportunity to return to their brigades, visiting and attending to the many advanced dressing stations that had been set up on the 28th and 29th. The Revd Canadine was to transfer from the MDS at Varennes to rejoin the Royal Sussex Pioneers in readiness to perform battlefield burials and to assist in connection with divisional salvage operations clearing dugouts of the dead. It can be seen that the chaplains were being deployed rapidly to fit in with changing battlefield conditions. On 5 November, Weston was pleased to report that the Revds Wheller and Bennet of the 54th Brigade had been awarded the MC. The fragment that survives from

A Church service before battle. (Author's collection)

the Revd Weston's diary ends in November, with the last entry perhaps being typical of the variety of tasks expected from chaplains in the division at the time. On 13 November the Revd Wheller was setting up a free soup kitchen for the men of the 54th Brigade and on the 18th the Revd Stopford was wounded in the leg while taking German prisoners to bring in the wounded.

The Revd E C Crosse believed that the growing practice of chaplains being closer to their men in time of battle had a good effect on the morale of both chaplains and men. As far as the chaplains were concerned "It was a great thing to think that the church was ready to go where the men had to go."[12] He thought that the significance of their presence on the battlefield was of great importance because "They alone were not under orders to be there, and as such could hardly fail to encourage the rest, who had no option in the matter."[13] The work of the chaplain near the front line consisted in helping at regimental aid posts, or leading stretcher-bearing parties, and locating the dead, making a careful note of where they had fallen if it was not possible to bring them in. Crosse places great importance on the work of chaplains both during and after the battle in discovering and identifying the dead, thus making the casualty lists more accurate. "It was worth almost any amount of labour to avoid reporting a man 'missing' unnecessarily".[14]

Crosse himself was involved with his battalions, the 8th and 9th Devons, on the first day of the Battle of the Somme at the attack on Mametz village from Mansel Copse.

He was stationed with the MO of the regiment at Wellington redoubt, but shortly after this initial attack went around the front line, "A journey around our front line revealed four badly wounded men in a dug out. I helped Hinton to drag them out and went for the stretcher bearers."[15] Later, with the MO, he walked down the road to Mansel Copse, where he found many more bodies. Crosse took command of the stretcher-bearers and spent the rest of the day clearing the battlefield. This continued on the 3rd and 4th,

An Army Chaplain tending British graves. (IWM Q4004)

culminating in the funeral at Mansel Copse. On Wednesday 12th he was at Caterpillar Trench, dealing with wounded and clearing the aid posts ready for more casualties.

In March 1916 the first VC to be awarded to a chaplain was won by the Revd Noel Mellish who was part of an attack on St Eloi on the 27th. Mellish distinguished himself by continuing to risk his life over several days at the height of the battle, bringing in the wounded. As we shall see, the posting of a chaplain to an ambulance was by no means a safe one and many chaplains were to be decorated for their refusal to leave wounded men in No Man's Land while there was a chance of getting them back alive.

1915 and 1916 had also seen chaplains in battle action on other fronts. The landings at Gallipoli, as we have seen, put an enormous strain on the department in the Middle East. At first, the Principal Chaplain, the Revd A W Horden, advised the chaplains that the best place for them would be at the advanced dressing station. This was at the earlier stages of the campaign when the number of chaplains was far fewer that it was to be later, and the main dilemma was the question was how the chaplains could be of the most use. However, he shortly changed his mind, as the Revd Oswin Creighton, with the 29th Division explained. "Operations on the Peninsula did not at all follow the book and later on the principal chaplain laid it down quite clearly, that … each chaplain must use his own discretion and be where he feels he can be of the greatest use."[16] The Roman Catholic chaplain, the Revd Finn, who thought his place was at the front line, landed with his troops at Suvla and was killed. Creighton had a different opinion.

> The chaplain is non-combatant and surely it must be wrong for him to go out in an attack, much though he may hate not to share the danger of his men to the full. His work comes after the attack.[17]

However, at the landing beaches it was difficult to make such distinctions and Creighton finds himself conducting services, tending to the wounded and trying to find the dead to bury them, all under shell fire from the Turkish army. Horden commented in his diary the opinion of the GOC Army Corps that "The chaplains have done splendidly; they are the admiration of everyone."[18]

The Bishop of Lahore described the difficulties in the disposition of his pathetically small band of chaplains in the battle for Kut in September 1915. The Revd Spooner was deployed with the British troops of General Delaine's division attacking on the left bank of the River Tigris. The Revd Bridge was placed at a Casualty Clearing Station and the Bishop himself went on the one boat available for picking up the wounded. He realised that his brief spell as a chaplain on active service did not qualify him to be an expert on disposition of chaplains in battle but he has some interesting things to say about the dilemmas faced:

> Certainly on a front like ours in Mesopotamia, the chances of ministering spiritually to the badly wounded or dying men on the field of battle or of administering to them the reserved sacrament were very hard to come by and perhaps we might have done worse than to take the line we did – namely to be about with the men, whether whole or wounded and as much as we could and be ready for any odd job that came along.[19]

His personal experience was of helping evacuate the wounded down the river in patrol boats and he obviously felt that his experience had brought him close to the men. "I shall be grateful all my life for the chance that ten days' nightmare voyage gave one of getting into close touch with the British soldier."[20] The Revd Harold Spooner, in the fall back on Kut, had volunteered to stay with a party of wounded and as a result of the courage shown in helping look after them was awarded the MC. He then joined the retreat and ended up in the siege of Kut where he started a regular routine of service and hospital rounds under increasingly difficult conditions as the siege continued. He describes how he visited the Oxfords in the first line trenches on Boxing Day 1915. "We got into the wrong trench and consequently got sniped pretty badly."[21] In Kut the distinction between the front line and behind the line was blurred as the whole place was subjected to heavy shelling from the Turkish troops. "Shells continually falling in on the hospital killing or wounding again those on the mend."[22] He went to visit the men in the trenches to wish them a Happy New Year and recalls looking through the loophole at the Turkish lines barely 30 yards away. Throughout the spring the battle around Kut raged, with Spooner recounting constant rumours of relieving forces being at hand. He continued his services and hospital visiting. He says of the troops, increasingly short of food and low in spirits "They are tired of hearing relief is coming." Of the services that Easter he said "I cannot explain the impressiveness of the services. All services are taken to the sound of the guns. I do not think hymns have ever been sung or prayers made with greater earnestness."[23] Eventually Kut was captured and Spooner remained as a chaplain to the prisoners of war, 1700 of whom died, despite the fact that he was offered the opportunity of returning home by the Red Cross. Spooner survived the war but suffered from his experiences in later life by having a complete mental breakdown that lasted many years.

Although the conditions and practicalities varied for chaplains of different fronts it can be seen that a common theme was the resolving of the dilemma of where the chaplain's role lay in battle conditions. Different chaplains responded in different ways, but all were trying to show the concern and love of God to their troops and to be useful in battle

Notes

1.   John Bickersteth, *The Bickersteth Diaries*, p. 83.
2.   Ibid, p. 91.
3.   Ibid, p. 93.
4.   Ibid, p. 106.
5.   William Drury, *Camp Follower*, p. 99.
6.   F.R. Barry, *Period of my Life*, p. 54.
7.   Drury, op. cit., p. 127.
8.   G.A.Weston, War Diary of the Senior Chaplain of the 18th Division (WO/95/2023).
9.   War Diary of 7th Battalion, Bedfordshire Regiment (WO/95/2043).
10. Weston op.cit.
11. Ibid.
12. E.C. Crosse Papers, IWM (80/22/1), p. 68.
13. Ibid., p. 70.
14. Ibid., p. 72.
15. Ibid.
16. O. Creighton, *With the Twenty-Ninth Division in Gallipoli*, p. 32.
17. Ibid., p. 32.
18. A.W. Horden, War Diary of the Principal Chaplain (WO/95/2023).

19. Bishop of Lahore, 'The R. A. Ch. D. in Mesopotamia', *Royal Army Chaplains' Department Quarterly Journal* Vol 2 No 7 (July 1923), pp.266-268.
20. Ibid.
21. H. Spooner Papers, IWM (1/51/94).
22. Ibid.
23. Ibid.

Chapter 4

Chaplains in hospitals and field ambulances

M uch of the work done by chaplains on the Western Front was concerned with the care of the wounded at base hospitals, ambulances and casualty clearing stations. When the first chaplains went out to France in 1914 they were often attached to field ambulances. This was the experience of the Revd Douglas Winnifrith who departed for France in August 1914 attached to the 14th Field Ambulance and also having the pastoral care of the 14th Infantry Brigade. The Revd Edmund Kennedy, a territorial chaplain who was called up and arrived on the Western Front in time to take part in the First Battle of Ypres, was attached to the 23rd Field Ambulance. The temporary chaplains were sometimes placed in base hospitals and then moved on, after some experience, to work with field ambulances. The Revd Charles Doudney wrote home, "As to my prospects, as far as I can see I will be called to the fighting zone in due course. It seems that they keep chaplains at base for a varying period and then send them more or less in order to the front – it has been hinted that my time will come soon."[1]

The work of chaplains at base hospitals was difficult in that they were ministering to a constantly changing congregation as men arrived and left regularly. Doudney is at first unsure on entering the large wards. "In some trepidation I enter the long ward, well knowing that in that ward there is at least an hour's work, work that demands one's very best, all one's manhood, tact, skill and knowledge of men."[2] He is humbled by the bravery of the men he ministers to. "The strong faith in looking forward to life as a cripple, the unflinching facing of the slow approach of death after the hope of recovery." He develops a routine of working his way down one side of the ward and up the other "they are waiting for you with a grin as you come around."[3] The Revd Sartell Prentice, an American Red Cross padre arriving at a large base hospital near St Nazaire, felt overwhelmed by his duties to start with. He found that the hospital authorities saw his duties as burials and dealing with hospital mail. He tried to see the 800-1300 men individually and found that his days had become a 'hodge podge' of many different tasks, none of them finished. He decided that, with the obvious exceptions of these who were seriously ill or in need of spiritual help, he would try and do something for the whole ward. He fell into a routine of being responsible for fetching the local newspaper and disseminating the war news by translating the articles. "Standing in the middle of the ward I translated the communiqués from the various fronts ... then would come questions and answers and perhaps a little discussion on the military situation."[4] He also organised YMCA concert parties and did personal shopping in town for those unable to leave their beds. When a hospital train arrived, he collected messages from the wounded to cable home and reassure their families. He also found it useful to be present in the operating theatre giving comfort and praying with those just about to go under the anaesthetic. He tells of administering Holy Communion both in large services and at beds. Faced with an impossible task, he had found his own way of ministering to a huge base hospital, by finding the best ways of being of both spiritual and practical help.

The Revd C. Doudney, Chaplain 6th Division. (Author's collection)

The Revd D Winnifrith was involved in the retreat from Mons, throughout which the field ambulance was never very far from the advancing German army. He bemoans the fact that it was not possible to hold services but makes himself useful in all sorts of ways. He was an experienced army chaplain and knew the importance of being in the thick of the action. He was busy finding food supplies for the ambulance unit and obtaining billets as well as rolling up his sleeves and tending to the wounded. He was deeply aware, however of his purely spiritual role, and that it was not confined to burying the dead. "I buried our dead whenever possible, but on the occasions when my duty to them and to the living clashed I felt it was more important that I should be with the latter"[5]

At the field ambulance at Jury in September he describes the scene. "At night we were especially busy. The ambulance bringing in as many as 150 men. As they lay in the straw … I went around and did what I could, taking a message for one, writing a card for another, giving drinks of Bovril and helping some to move into a more comfortable position, saying a word to all and having prayers with the most serious cases."[6] He expresses continually the sense of his work being a mix of the practical and the spiritual.

In these earlier days of the war the chaplains working with the field ambulances were very close to action and the dilemma of whether a chaplain should be in the fighting areas does not seem to have been a question given much consideration. The field ambulance kept up communication with the regimental aid posts in the front line and the casualty clearing stations to the rear. Casualties were received firstly in the regimental aid post and then transferred to the ambulance. Winnifrith explains how the men working to complete the transfers were often under fire – "In this campaign, with its constant artillery duels between long range guns, the field ambulance had been constantly under shell fire. The journeys between dressing station and aid posts have always been perilous."[7] He continues, "I have often accompanied these expeditions and have therefore first hand knowledge of the difficulties and dangers they involved."[8]

The winter of 1915 found Winnifrith in the Ypres sector and found him quite often called upon to take the journey to the front line to bury casualties. The brigade was holding an extended line and as a consequence. "The journeys each night to fetch the wounded were long and arduous."[9] The Revd Edmund Kennedy was also in the Ypres sector in the winter of 1915. We saw in Chapter 2 how he had come under fire and had ridden over Hill 60 to deliver an important message. In his memoir of his time in France he puts forward his philosophy on the role of the chaplain and immediately after 'taking services' comes 'comforting the dying'. He had strong views about the value of the presence of a padre amongst the severely wounded. "If the dying man is conscious and realised his position, then there will be the last messages for the loved ones at home ... the setting right of some existing wrong"[10] This work entailed a great deal of time on the part of the chaplain. He had a wide concept of the role of the chaplain in the field ambulance that included dealing with correspondence for the wounded, carrying messages and tending to the wounded in exposed places. He visited an advanced dressing station. "Their condition is indescribable and opportunities for a word of comfort abound ... The message of God, coupled sometimes with so material a solace of placing a cigarette between the lips of the sufferer, will help him to bear the agony."[11] He has a simple reply for those who ask "Should a chaplain be under fire?" He says "It is impossible to avoid it if he is serving troops under fire and he must take his chance with everyone else."[12] Doudney, with the 18th Infantry Brigade near Ypres in October 1915, travelled up to the front line trenches regularly. He wrote to his home parish "Today I was up for nearly six hours and had a

Chaplain with Ambulance unit. (IWM Q1222)

great deal of hiding in dug-outs and dodging out to take funerals."[13] On 13 October he hitched a lift with an officer from the 18th Field Ambulance to go to a regimental aid post to conduct a funeral. On the way, at a crossroads just outside Ypres the vehicle came under shellfire and Doudney was injured. The stomach wound proved fatal and he died on the 16 October.

The Revd Oswin Creighton in Gallipoli was finding his feet as a chaplain with the 29th Division by June 1915. He described his work with the 88th and 89th Field Ambulances. In the battles in the first week of June his regiment, the Royal Fusiliers, suffered heavy losses. He visited the 88th Dressing Station up the gully from gully beach. "I cannot imagine anything much more blood curdling than to go up the gully for the first time when a fierce battle is raging." But he is still constrained by orders from a chaplain senior to him. "I went right up to the head of the gully to an advanced post of the 87th and found that the R.F.'s dressing station had gone right up to their support trenches, where H. had been so emphatic that it was not to go. I am quite sure this was just the place I should have been."[14]

The Revd E C Crosse explains how the role of the chaplain was changing by the end of 1915. He describes how it was argued that it had been generally felt that one of the primary roles of the chaplain was to visit the sick and minister to the dying, hence the usual placing of the chaplain, at least initially, with the field ambulance. As the line became more fixed and static, the role of the field ambulances changed. Crosse explains,

> Field ambulances became little more than dressing stations … The great object of the field ambulance was to evacuate its wounded with the greatest possible speed

A Chaplain assisting in bringing in the wounded. (IWM Q5626)

and the few who were kept ... were expected to recover in a few days. Once again it seemed that the padre's sphere was getting narrower, and whereas in 1914 there was generally quite enough to keep him busy, at the end of 1915 the doctors were beginning to regard him as rather a nuisance.[15]

Crosse uses these opinions as part of his argument that the proper place for chaplains was ministering to the fit and well in the front line just about to go over the top.

As preparations for the Battle of the Somme progressed however, the organisation and plans for the disposition of chaplains in battle became more definite and organised and still based primarily around the field ambulance and advanced aid posts. The practice became more widespread of the senior chaplain appointing battle positions to all the chaplains in his division. One of the ambulances in the division was the main dressing station, behind the line and the other two would be attached to the attacking brigades. Each of these would be divided into a dressing station and an advanced dressing station. Two chaplains would be attached to the main dressing station and one each to the other two. The remaining chaplains were given permission to accompany the troops into the firing line.

It was usual for the chaplains who went into battle to work with the battalion M.O. Some stayed throughout at the regimental aid post; where there was almost certain to be a great congestion of work ... if he wished to the padre could accompany stretcher bearers in their very difficult work of locating the wounded who could not walk. Every M.O. was so hopelessly overworked in battle that he was sure to welcome such help ... it can be easily recognised that under such circumstances a great alliance often sprung up between the padre and the M.O. to both of whom it was given the privilege not of adding to the wounds of battle but of relieving them.[16]

The recognition that chaplains needed to be assigned specific battle positions seemed to be widespread in 1916. By 24 September 1916 the 18th Division DHQ was at Hedauville. The division was getting into position for the assault on Thiepval Village and Schwaben Redoubt. The war diary of the Revd G Weston, Senior Chaplain of the 18th Division, sheds some light on the role of the chaplains in the battle for the Somme. In preparation for this attack the chaplains of the 55th Brigade, Boddingtons and Stopford, were detached from their regiments and attached to the dressing station at Clairfaye Farm "in readiness for the expected battle." The Revd Canadine was similarly reassigned to the MDS 54th Field Ambulance at Varennes. The chaplains of the 54th and 53rd Brigades were notified that they were to be responsible for all areas east of Hedauville and were to be based at Aveluy Post and Wood Post. In his diary of 26 September the Senior Chaplain of the division, the Revd G Weston, reports the attack which resulted in the capture of Thiepval. He had that day ridden to visit the chaplains working at the ADS at Aveuly Post and Black Horse Ridge. He gives some detail about the deployment of his chaplains at various aid posts and at Clairfaye Farm. The Revds Bodington and Stopford had been at Clairfaye Farm "working two days and nights." They had been "taking charge of arrangements for walking wounded" and also "giving individual attention to the spiritual and other needs of the wounded." Generally, he had concluded, they had been giving assistance "in any way open to them."[17] The Revd R Wheller, who was with the 12th Middlesex, had been wounded by a gunshot wound to his arm but had remained on duty. 27 September found Weston reporting that "Battle conditions are still prevailing." The chaplains had been performing some battlefield funerals and still had "much work at dressing stations." The war diary of the 55th Field Ambulance based at Clairfaye Farm where chaplains Boddington and Stopford were based, reported 2,114 other ranks casualties and 60 officer casualties pass through from 26 September to 4 October.[18] The 54th Field Ambulance was based at Varennes and by midnight on the 29th had seen over 600 stretcher cases since the 26th.[19] Entries in Weston's diary show the chaplains working with the field ambulances and dressing stations and providing for the spiritual and practical needs of the units that they were attached to.

There is no doubt that it was in their work at ambulances and advanced dressing stations that chaplains showed their commitment to the need of their men by performing acts of bravery in bringing in wounded. The papers of Bishop Gwynne contain press cuttings from national papers with many reports of chaplains being commended and decorated for acts of bravery. Gwynne has collected these cuttings and also kept notes of many individual chaplains. In two examples among the many, Gwynne comments on the Revd Guy Rogers who won an MC in November 1916 and quotes his citation "For conspicuous gallantry and devotion to duty in action. He worked ceaselessly all night under fire, tending and carrying in the wounded."[20] Also the Revd Basil Plumtree who was killed in July 1916, having won an MC "For gallantry and devotion when attached to a dressing station. He rendered great assistance in dressing the wounded and assisted to bring in the wounded under heavy shell fire."[21]

The Bishop of Lahore, writing in the *Royal Army Chaplains' Department Journal* in 1923, described the situation in Mesopotamia in the days leading up to and during the advance on Kut in September 1915. The expeditionary force was fighting 300 miles from base and the Bishop was with the many casualties being evacuated down the river by P boat to Basra. He describes conditions on the 'P4'.

> There were two doctors, men whose utter devotion I shall remember all my life, and one nursing orderly; so the padre had to take off his coat and keep it off and give

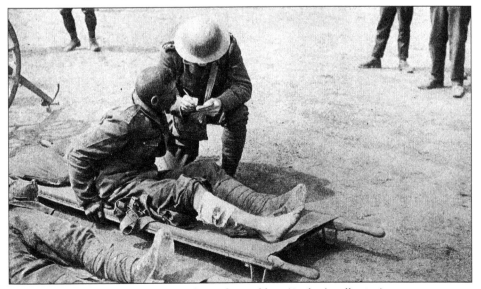

A Chaplain writing home for a soldier. (Author's collection)

himself to doing what an untrained man could do to help the experts in caring for the suffering.[22]

Siegfried Sassoon's autobiographical character, George Sherston, described the scene in a dressing station and is damning of an Anglican chaplain he encounters who, he says, "was painfully aware that he could do nothing except stand around and feel sympathetic. The consolations of the Church of England weren't much in demand."[23] Although this character is fictional, the sentiments expressed sum up the attitude of Sassoon to the Anglican chaplains. The evidence from men and chaplains under battle conditions completely contradicts this, showing how chaplains working with hospitals and field ambulances were both brave and useful. Many of the MCs awarded to chaplains in the war were for gallantry in the course of their practical efforts in bringing in wounded and spiritual care of wounded in ambulances and hospitals. Although both contemporary and modern commentators have described the worth of the chaplain being measured by being seen to be in the thick of the action, much valuable work was being done by chaplains at dressing stations and hospitals which consisted of medical, social and spiritual work and did not preclude the opportunity of courage in battle situations being shown by the chaplains on many occasions.

Notes

1.   Jonathan Horne, *The Best of Good Fellows*, p. 122.
2.   Ibid, p. 113.
3.   Ibid, p. 114.
4.   S. Prentice, *Padre*, p.79
5.   D.P. Winnifrith, *The Church in the Fighting Line*, p. 87.
6.   Ibid, p. 83.
7.   Ibid, p. 145.
8.   Ibid, p. 16.
9.   Ibid, p. 17.
10. E. Kennedy, *With The Immortal Seventh Division*, p. 145.
11. Ibid, p. 146.
12. Ibid, p. 149.
13. Horne, op. cit., p. 169.
14. O. S. Greighton, *With the 29th Division in Gallipoli*, p. 121.
15. E. C. Crosse Papers, IWM (80/22/1), p. 53.
16. Ibid, p. 71.
17. G. A. Weston. War Diary of the Senior Chaplain to the 18th Division (WO95/2023).
18. The War Diaries of the 55th Field Ambulance (WO95/2030).
19. The War Diaries of the 54th Field Ambulance (WO95/2031).
20. L. H. Gwynne, *Army Book*.
21. Ibid.
22. Bishop of Lahore, 'The R. A. Ch. D. in Mesopotamia', *Royal Army Chaplains' Department Quarterly Journal* Vol 2 No 7 (July 1923), pp.266-268.
23. Siegfried Sassoon, *The Memoirs of George Sherston*, quoted by A. Wilkinson, *The Church of England in the First World* War, p. 113.

Chapter 5

Services

Notwithstanding the complexities and difficulties of the chaplain's role at the front one duty that seemed to be certain to the new chaplain was that of taking services. This however proved to be the most frustrating as well as the most rewarding part of his job. The difficulties of providing services to all units in the battle area were immense and although, as time went on, the organisation of the Chaplains' Department developed to deal with this challenge, there were still units of troops separated from the main battalion, artillery units for example, who were not often blessed with a service.

Often well-laid plans for services on a Sunday were disrupted by sudden changes of plan for troop movements. The Revd D Winnifrith notes during the Battle of the Aisne "The early celebration and morning service I had arranged had to be cancelled at the last minute in consequence of my brigade being called on to assist in repelling a threatened attack by the enemy."[1] Again at la Basse, "My programmes for Sunday were so frequently disturbed in this way that probable moves have come to be associated with me. Often I had it said of me "Now padre, don't fix up services for next Sunday or we shall be moved.[2] Neville Talbot described the difficulties as "hens trying to lay eggs on moving staircases."[3] Harry Blackburne recalls how he had to take to task, in his capacity as Assistant Chaplain General, a brigadier who was constantly cancelling brigade services.[4]

Trying to provide Sunday service to all the units he was responsible for was a problem and for the average chaplain in charge of two battalions providing the service necessitated a great deal of travel on a Sunday. The Revd E C Crosse tells us "It was quite common to take three parade services in a morning with an early morning communion service and a voluntary service in the evening."[5] Duff Crerar describes how, for chaplains, Sundays became a hectic race "as padres realised that nothing could sour the … soldiers attitude to parades sooner than to keep them waiting."[6]

The basic building block of religious service in the army was the church parade. Controversy raged over the usefulness, particularly the spirituality of the service throughout the war, with men, officers, generals and padres all contributing to the differences of opinion as to its function and purpose. The main objection from the ranks was the association of the service with kit and uniform inspection and the fact that attendance was compulsory. Whatever religious feeling was present at the outset was overcome by resentment at the necessity to be "spick and span" and the suspicion that, in the eye of the authorities, the service was an excuse to perform this inspection. Often this resentment ran so deep that any chance of a religious atmosphere was doomed from the start. Duff Crerar quotes the *Canadian Churchman* of November 1918:

> There is certainly more discipline than divinity about a church parade. The men have to turn out shaved and spotless with gleaming buttons belts and badges. All this means work … this is the prelude to divine service. When all these disciplinary measures have been carried out the men are marched to church, where they are more often than not preached 'at' or talked to in a way that would be an insult to the intelligence of an Eskimo.[7]

Michael Snape has described the situation:

Although it was technically possible to declare oneself an atheist, agnostic, or a member of any obscure denomination in order to avoid parade services in practice there was no alternative for the refractory save the prospect of long and unpleasant fatigues.

Even regular churchgoers in the army were divided in their opinions. Snape continues:

... while some of those who were church members and church goers in civilian life cherished the fact that their ability to attend public worship was safeguarded by the army, others, including some chaplains, felt that the principle of compulsion and the chore of inspections discredited the churches and was counter-productive in religious terms.[8]

Frank Richards claims that church parade was "thoroughly detested".[9] However there is evidence that for some the parade services were appreciated and fulfilled some useful purpose. Although some of the written evidence is damning of church parades Schweitzer points out that in diaries and letters there is often confusion about terms describing services – "For many other soldiers 'services' mean reverent occasions whereas "Church Parades" connote mundane compulsory events."[10] Others make a point of distinguishing between church parades and other services in their accounts of their spiritual life at the front. Sapper Percy Ram, after fulminating about the church parade he had been forced to attend goes on to say that "he enjoyed the service in the evening which I attended voluntarily."[11] Julian Bickersteth in July 1916 says "I am becoming less and less enamoured of the compulsory church parade. I think we shall do far better work as chaplains by insisting on the voluntary service."[12] Harry Blackburne, however, who had been an army chaplain since 1903 had a more robust view of the parade services:

Parade services are the normal thing. We have at times to deal with those who are opposed to all types of compulsory services – that is not to say that the men do not like such services. They dislike the many preparations they have to make. I do not believe the dislike goes further than that. I am convinced that parade services ought not to be allowed to fall into disuse.[13]

Some chaplains felt the parade services were the only opportunity to address the whole unit and were willing to put up with its imperfections in order to preach to men who would otherwise not have had any contact with the church at the front. Such views are possibly the triumph of hope over experience, as Duff Crerer points out, "Chaplains were rarely willing to admit that under such circumstances any hope of a fair hearing presumed extraordinary divine intervention".[14] Blackburne, however, has some advice on the skills needed to make the parade a success – "Use a normal voice, not a clerical voice. Have something to say and say it as if you mean it."[15] He recommended the breaking of the square to form a semi-circle, which he believed to be more "friendly and homely". He had managed by August 1917 to have this procedure regularised by his army commander. He comments "I have done this for a long time with the consent of the senior officer on parade but now it can be done by all chaplains because it has the army commander's approval."[16] E C Crosse also seems to have had a more optimistic view of the way chaplains could deal with the problem of church parades:

> On active service nearly all COs were over the course of time persuaded to dissociate from divine service the countless inspections which make it unpopular in peacetime soldiering. Generally speaking it became the custom for troops to be paraded for divine service in clean fatigue dress and the padre who knew his business could usually see that the company commanders who made the service an opportunity for inspection was brought to see the error of his ways.[17]

Crosse often emphasises in his writing the importance of the chaplain's role that, he felt, was necessary to maintain the status of the chaplains in the army structure. He seems to have been willing to go ahead with church parades, albeit under his own terms, in order to both have an opportunity to speak to all the men and also to keep the profile of religion high. "After all the service was a military rather than an ecclesiastical institution and it was essential that the padre should remember that … those who did could do an enormous amount to vindicate religion in the eyes of the army." His principle was "At all times to treat the men as though they had come to the service of their own accord." Evidence from the Revd L Jeeves writing in January 1916 shows that the length and content of the service were not too onerous:

> The service lasted about 25 minutes and included three hymns, a shortened form of prayer with the creed and the last 6 verses of the 81st psalm and a sermon lasting 7 or 8 minutes. Then came 'The King' and the blessing.[19]

A Service attended by King George V on his visit to the
Western Front, April 1915. (Author's collection)

The debate over the usefulness and validity of church parades continued to exercise chaplains during the war and after. The success the chaplain had in mitigating the unpleasant aspects of the parade seems to have depended to quite a degree on where they were stationed, and both Julian Bickersteth and Noel Mellish describe how they more or less gave up on church parades but nevertheless found that attendance at voluntary services remained high.

Much more rewarding to the chaplains were the voluntary services held after parade and at various other times. They were considered to be of much more worth and significance than the parade service. Holy Communion or Holy Eucharist was seen as an essential part of the padre's ministry. Although mainstream Anglicanism did not place as much emphasis on the sacraments as the Roman Catholic Church, the Holy Eucharist, since the growth of the Tractarian Movement in the Anglican Church, was seen as the most significant and worthwhile service. The personal memoirs of serving Anglican chaplains are peppered with accounts of preparing men for confirmation so that they could take part in the sacrament. Bishop Gwynne's wartime diaries show a considerable amount of his time was spent in touring the Western Front confirming candidates that had been prepared by their brigade or divisional chaplain. As attendance at Holy Communion service was not compulsory and often took place in addition to and after parade service, attendance figures were a more clear indication to the chaplains of the strength of religious feeling in their units. The memorial of Christ's sacrifice on the cross struck a chord with those who were about to offer their lives in battle and the celebration of communion was described by the chaplains in terms which recognised this. The Revd John White commented on communion services near the front:

> Within the sound of guns and in a hall that had been shattered by shells, it is a very solemn service. The meaning of divine suffering and sacrifice stood out with a new plainness and one understood … that the need of man is just this fellowship with the suffering of him who had shed his blood for our sins.[20]

Chaplains had to revise some of their long held beliefs about the administration of communion. It was realised that the tradition of a 'fasting' communion made no sense when services were often quickly arranged and had to fit in with army routine. Those who had previously objected to the use of the reserved sacrament realised its usefulness under battle conditions. Blackburne was in the lead in this more flexible attitude, cheerfully asserting not long after he arrived in France, "We have communion services at all times of the day and night. One has to change one's ideas out here."[21] The Revd Wyteland, writing to the vicar of Stoke Bishop, talks about the difficulty of holding to any kind of liturgical regime and the need to be flexible:

> On Good Friday I helped at six consecutive services. For each we had a parade service followed by Holy Communion. 250 stayed for the Blessed Sacrament. For many of them it was their last. We made it an Easter service, prematurely in date but not surely in any other way.[22]

One of the criticisms levelled at chaplains in the First World War is that they did not write much about their spiritual work, but there are many mentions of Holy Communion and the satisfaction chaplains felt at taking a well-attended communion service. Julian Bickersteth was a great advocate of as many communion services as possible, feeling that

"We have fed the hungry with matins and evensong for generations, when all the time they were hungering … for the bread of life."[23] He describes an outdoor communion service with which the weather played havoc, but nothing could take away the deep impressiveness of the service or the devotion and reverence of the men.[24] At Talbot House many men and officers took communion in the beautiful and peaceful setting of the 'upper room'. Tubby Clayton spoke of the atmosphere of the chapel "The homely beauty of the chapel, with its inward gift of hope and fellowship drew many who learnt their hunger in the grimmest school."[25] On Easter Day 1916 there were ten celebrations of Holy Communion from 5.30 am. Many of the men, freshly confirmed, made their first and last communion in the upper room.

Informal services, held in barns, dugouts and fields, became an increasing part of the chaplain's work. Informality of procedure and language became the order of the day. The Revd Milner-White in *The Church in the Furnace*, comments "liturgy vanished with peace and rubrics paled in a redder world. An immense spontaneous amicable anarchy has sprung up and this has been the church in the furnace."[26] Milner-White has criticisms to make about the Book of Common Prayer, describing its use at the front as "semi-usable and semi-used."[27] He describes parade service as mangled matins, but is faced with the difficulty that matins and evensong are the only forms of service universally known to the men. The morning and evening offices of the church were condensed and refined around the main elements of the Creed, Lord's Prayer and confession. Milner-White believed that the singing of hymns was a popular and useful part of the services at the front,

Funeral service at Etaples Camp. (IWM Q11033)

Singing has a worth impossible to exaggerate ... careful watching has convinced me that a hymn mediates to an Englishman another country ... it is his chosen sacrament of approach to God.[28]

Chaplains were also trying to deliver their services in a more user-friendly manner. Blackburne was a great opponent of the 'parsonical voice' and Milner-White comments on the need for a sharper delivery. "As for the chaplains, they have forgotten all that slumberous ease which so easily attaches itself to the recitation of an office and learned that every prayer and sentence needs effort and care."[29]

Chaplains increasingly found that services nearer the line had to be arranged more informally and in smaller groups to avoid becoming targets. The Revd Winnifrith often spent the second half of his Sundays finding small groups of men who had not been able to attend a service behind the lines. He held services for small groups of men in dugouts or behind hedges and in barns. The Revd E Kennedy thought that these impromptu, informal gatherings, sometimes in small billets near the line were of more spiritual value than more formal occasions. The GOC of 101st Infantry Brigade describes how a brigade chaplain, the Revd W G. Burgis, "spent the night in the trenches, to cheer them up and conduct short services."[30] Doudney talks of seeking out isolated groups of artillery men who had not seen a padre for a while and conducting informal services. "These are the services I like best."[31] Many of the first-hand accounts of the chaplains and officers bear witness to the flexibility and resourcefulness of the chaplains in taking services far removed from the often disliked parade services.

On other fronts, many of the same problems and practicalities affected the taking of services. Before the advance on Kut in Sept 1915 the Bishop of Lahore describes a large service outdoors: "The whole force formed in a hollow square. I shall never forget that simple little evensong ... I know from what fellows told me afterwards that a great many men got in touch with the unseen."[32] During the few days leading up to the battle it was discovered that there were twenty men and officers who were wanting to be confirmed and it was decided to go ahead without preparation and hope that the candidates would survive to catch up later.

The Revd Spooner, in the siege of Kut in Mesopotamia in the winter and spring of 1915–16, struggled to provide adequate services to the besieged troops under constant shelling and a Turkish attack. Early in January 1916 he conducted a communion service in the trenches near the Turkish lines "About 20 communicants, mostly officers. We sang two Christmas hymns – it seemed to mean a great deal to these men facing death daily, sometimes hourly."[33]

Conditions in Gallipoli were not conducive to the taking of services as the Principal Chaplain, The Revd Horden reports in his war diary "The difficulties are very great as no part of the peninsula is free from shell fire."[34] The Revd Oswin Creighton tells of a service on the eve of Ascension Day, in wet conditions:

It cleared up ... enough for me to be able to hold a service in an adjoining field for the Lancashire Fusiliers and the Royal Fusiliers to which several officers and and a number of men came. But the battle began just about that time and raged very fiercely over our heads.[35]

On Ascension Day he had more luck and was able to hold a communion service as a remembrance for those who had been killed in the two regiments. On the following

Sunday heavy shell fire stopped his morning service taking place and he decided to visit his men in the trenches, eventually finding a group of Lancashire Fusiliers who were pleased to have a service, and later took a service for the Royal Dublin Fusiliers high up on the side of the cliff.[36]

A major part of the chaplains' services were, of course, the conducting of funerals. In the early days of the war, during and after the retreat from Mons, during lulls in the battle, chaplains were able to find the wounded and mark graves with personal crosses. Winnifrith gives a touching account of the burial of a motorcycle messenger in the village churchyard. But as trench warfare developed, burials became more rushed and dangerous affairs, often performed under fire. Chaplains adapted the funeral service to suit the circumstances. Millner White condones this, criticising the burial service as it appears in the Book of Common Prayer. He says of the service "The present one has failed badly in the day of death."[37] The individual changes made by chaplains resulted in his opinion in "An office no less beautiful but far more human."[38] The Revd Hood relates a funeral service in the trenches in Gallipoli just as dawn was breaking "no light or book, so by heart I used what prayers seemed most useful ending with the one that invites the whole church in paradise and earth".[39]

As we have seen the chaplains made special efforts and took pride in providing services for the major religious festivals. Many chaplains' accounts of the war include detailed descriptions of the nature and number of services attended on Christmas Day and Easter Sunday. On Christmas Day in Kut the Revd Spooner set out to the second line trenches to take a communion service.

> What an extraordinary service! 18 officers and men in a dugout. A milk box for an altar … a flask for a chalice … ordinary plate for a paten, bullets whizzing overhead.

A burial service at Baghdad. (IWM 25260)

We sang two hymns, *While shepherds watched their flocks* and *Hark the herald angels sing.* Never have I heard such devout and earnest singing, never have I seen a congregation so thoughtful and devout.[40]

In April 1915 the Bishop of London, the Right Revd Wittington Ingram, visited the Western Front and was impressed by the response of the men and officers at the various services he held along the front line and at base hospitals and camps. The officer who was detailed to accompany him described one of the Easter Day services:

Strange though the surroundings were, with guns firing and the crack of rifles distinctly heard one would doubt a more reverent congregation has ever been gathered together on Easter Sunday morning, or if the meaning of the great central service of the Christian Church could ever be more clearly realised or the sacred presence more clearly felt.[41]

The bishop himself thought that the visit had been a great success and commented on the number of troops attending and the reverent atmosphere.

The task of providing services for the troops throughout the war was one that was of high priority to the Chaplains' Department. They may have failed in scope and nature of the services supplied, but the evidence in their writings shows how unremittingly they worked to provide these services in a wide variety of circumstances.

Notes

1.   D. Winnifrith, *The Church in the Fighting Line*, p.94.
2.   Ibid, p.133.
3.   Alan Wilkinson, *The Church of England in the First World War*, p.144.
4.   H. Blackburne, *This also Happened on the Western Front*, p.118.
5.   E.C. Crosse Papers, IWM (80/22/1)
6.   Duff Crerar, *Padres in No Man's Land*, p.98.
7.   Ibid, p.93.
8.   Michael Snape, *God and the British Soldier*, p.140.
9.   Frank Richards, *Old Soldiers Never Die*, p.84.
10.   Richard Schweizter, *The Cross and the Trenches*, p.200.
11.   Ibid, p.201.
12.   J. Bickersteth (ed), *The Bickersteth Diaries*, p.116.
13.   H Blackburne, Papers, RAChD archives.
14.   Crerar, op. cit., p.93.
15.   Blackburne, op. cit.
16.   Ibid.
17.   Crosse, op. cit., p.23
18.   Ibid. p.24
19.   L. Jeeves, papers, IWM docs (80/22/1)
20.   John White, *With the Cameronians in France*, p.8.
21.   Blackburne, op. cit., p.16.
22.   Diaries and papers of Bishop Llewelyn Henry Gwynne (XACC/18/Z/1 Army Book).
23.   Bickersteth, op. cit., p.82.
24.   Ibid, p.131.
25.   P.Clayton, *Tales of Talbot House*, p.78.

26. E. Milner-White, in F. B. Macnutt, *The Church in the Furnace,* p.175.
27. Milner-White in Macnutt, op. cit., p.177.
28. Ibid, p.196.
29. Ibid. p.176
30. Bishop Llewelyn Henry Gwynne, op.cit.
31. Jonathon Horne, *The Best of Good Fellows,* p.144.
32. Bishop of Lahore, 'The R. A. Ch. D. in Mesopotamia', *Royal Army Chaplains' Department Quarterly Journal* Vol 2 No 7 (July 1923), pp.266-268.
33. H. Spooner Papers, IWM (1/51/94).
34. A.W. Horden, The War Diary of the Principal Chaplain (WO/ 95/203)
35. O. Creighton, *With the Twenty-Ninth Division in Gallipoli,* p. 89.
36. Ibid, p.99.
37. Milner-White, op. cit., p.175.
38. Milner White, op., cit. p.179
39. Ibid, p.181
40. Spooner, op. cit,
41. *The Times,* 12 April 1915
42. *The Times,* 12 April 1915

Chapter 6

Holy Grocery

Geoffrey Gordon starts his contribution to *Papers from Picardy*, 'The Chaplain's Dilemma', with the following anecdote:

> Somewhere in England: A young curate is passing down a mean street of the town. Two children are playing in the gutter ... As he passes, the curate overhears their conversation:
>
> Do you know 'oo that is? I knows 'im, that's Mr God that is!
>
> Mr God – a burdensome title but ... at the same time it is real encouragement to the young curate to know that there are some people to whom he is indeed the representative of God. Somewhere in France the chaplain is walking down the narrow streets of a town which for many months has been one of the bases for the British army. A crowd of children of all ages leave their play and run up to him as he comes.
>
> M. Cinema! Cinema Ce soir?
>
> Laissez-moi venir.
>
> Non, M. Cinema, pas lui M – mais moi – c'est ma mere qui fait votre ligne.
>
> Au revoir M Cinema. A ce soir, M Charlie Chaplain.[1]

Mr God or M. Cinema, which does the chaplain stand for? One of the most frequent criticisms of the chaplain in the Great War, at the time and subsequently, was that one of his chief functions seemed to be the supplier of material wants and entertainment to the troops. Neville Talbot, Senior Chaplain to the 56th Division, called this 'Holy Grocery' and the term has become synonymous with the idea that instead of concentrating on spiritual growth and revival in the trenches, the chaplains got diverted into becoming some kind of social workers, creating canteens and procuring cinema shows and concert parties. Even the nickname of one of the most famous Anglican army chaplains, Geoffrey Studdert Kennedy, 'Woodbine Willie', has given credence to the idea that the chaplains were suppliers of vast quantities of cigarettes and material comforts.

Stephen Louden, in his study of the chaplains' role in the army since 1914, has been very critical of the Anglican army chaplains in the First World War. He considered that they suffered from having an imprecisely defined role. "There are numerous examples of clergy engaging in activities which, while not inimical to their role as chaplain, are only peripherally connected with what was generally considered to be a clergyman's role."[2] The chaplains, according to Louden, were overanxious to be useful to the detriment of their spiritual duties.

> Out of the line in those earlier and more ill-directed days there were the compulsory church parades, the relentless call for organized sport, the running of the inevitable canteen, while in the frantic turmoil and confusion of battle, first aid to the wounded, reverent attendance upon the last rites of the fallen and hurried and heartbreaking

correspondence with the bereaved at home crowded out all other demands on a padre's time and energies.[3]

Louden takes this quotation from Duncan Blair, a padre with a Scottish regiment, and uses similar accounts, for example, the Revd Charles Doudney's description of a day spent helping with X-ray machines as proof that "The specifically religious activities of chaplains took second place."[4] He is particularly scathing about the Revd Harry Blackburne's accounts of providing tea to troops in the Battle of Loos:

> One may legitimately wonder what the Quartermaster's Department were doing, and may confidently assume that they were neither praying or acting as a locum for the chaplain.[5]

The dilemma in which chaplains found themselves as to the real nature of their ministry to the troops was one that did not escape them at the time. Contemporary accounts written by chaplains on active service are full of references to the situation in which they found themselves. They were often considered by company commanders to have plenty of spare time that could be filled usefully by organising football matches, censoring letters or setting up a canteen. The Revd F R Barry described the situation in the earlier days of the war: "The Chaplains' job was to take church parades, to run entertainments, to help in censoring letters and in general to act as welfare officers."[5] Later, when it had been established that the padres had work to do in the front line he mentions the topic of cigarettes.

> We did what we could to serve them in Christ's name – and surely the distribution of cigarettes was the relevant form of the cup of cold water – and they understood this was why we were doing it. They did not regard us just as welfare officers. In some dim way they discovered that they needed what the ministry of the church had to offer.[7]

The Revd Charles Doudney, in a sermon preached while on home leave in July 1915, spoke of an article he had read in a daily paper about chaplains at the front that divided chaplains into three kinds. Firstly there were the ones who concentrated mainly on "the exact nature of the service and on what robes to wear." Then there were the ones who spent time looking after the troops with material comforts, writing letters and providing cigarettes. The third type were the "missionaries, filled with the highest possible ideal which they at all time hold before the men who are fighting." Doudney says that he has come across some chaplains of the first two types but that,

> ... nearly all I have met belong, most decidedly and definitely, to the class of missionaries who do not rest until they have brought the highest possible ideal into the hearts of the brave men who are fighting. Certainly we do try and help with the writing of letters and in the concert and games, but this is apart from our real work, which is to deliver the message of the other world.[8]

Accounts of their work in all areas of the front, in the line, at base camp and at field hospital contain descriptions of the work carried out for the material benefit and raised morale of troops but these accounts are always accompanied by soul searching and justification for these roles as well as a realisation that perhaps a more overtly religious role is also necessary. Julian Bickersteth, Senior Chaplain of the 56th Division:

> My recreation room is really successful and very popular. We take 40-50 francs a day selling 1d cups of tea and 1d pieces of cake. The library is made use of to the full ... yet to get down underneath to the spiritual needs of the men, to get them to awake to the great truths of Christianity – this is a work which only a few can achieve – and mind you that is our real work.[9]

This does not seem to be a comfortable or self-delusional attitude to the comparative roles of chaplains. Indeed, he saw a real need for the chaplain to work hard behind the line to provide recreational facilities. On a visit to Arras he described a visit to a soldiers' club set up by a newly arrived chaplain. "He has only been a fortnight in town and already turned the large underground vaults cellars and chambers of the Archbishops' Palace into a first rate canteen, writing room and concert hall."[10] In his introduction to *Somewhere in Flanders* Stuart John Maclaren describes the work of the Revd Samuel Leighton Green:

> He was also expected to contribute to the raising of morale – almost anything that made life more tolerable, tinned fruit, jam, camp coffee, biscuits, bootlaces ... were in short supply. Green soon became an expert scrounger and friend of all the nearby quartermasters.[11]

He also asked friends back at St Barnabas to start a fag-mag fund to enable these essentials to be sent to his troops. When Green moved to be chaplain of the 1/4 Battalion, London Division, again he was active in raising morale by supplying material goods.

Chaplain helping old woman. (IWM Q10888)

An important element in morale was the canteen, which he was tireless in his efforts to supply with palatable food and cigarettes. Another was the battalion orchestra that he encouraged, and helped organise the divisional concert parties known as the 'Bow Bells'. However, by far the largest concerns that he writes about to his home congregation are the work he does in ministering to the dying, and the provision of church services to the living. The Revd Lachlan MacLean Watt, Chaplain to the Gordon Highlanders and the Black Watch says of the chaplain:

> He is not, if he be a true man … an anaemic imitation officer with a clerical collar on. He has to be a comrade to all, friend of the weary helper of the weak and light bringer in the dark hour. He may be mess president, leader and share of a quip and crank at the officers' tables, and purveyor of amusements at the camp, but if his work stops there it is not half began.[12]

The Revd Horsley Smith says:

> A chaplain's real work did not consist of giving out cigarettes, nor even bringing in the wounded under fire but in ministering the word and sacraments and often standing in the eyes of men as a link with home and other things which were 'lovely and of good report'.

He is scornful of the idea that the distribution of cigarettes was essential to establishing contact with the men. He recalls how he was told "You will need some cigarettes to distribute, the men won't look at you unless you have." He says "I felt this was wrong and proved that it was."[13]

The Revd Geoffrey Gordon writes at length on the way the chaplain is caught between the two stools of spirituality and much-needed material and social work. He sees this as being a dilemma that applies much more when the unit the chaplain is serving with is at base or a quiet section of the trenches. In battle, he believes the chaplain is often busy helping with blankets and stretchers while always alert to the possibility of being able to "put in a word of more articulate religion."[14] When his unit is behind the lines he has a choice:

> Either he will elect to stand strongly, definitely and exclusively for spiritual things in which case he will have to content himself with coming into contact with very few men, or in order to get to know the battalion as a whole he will have to throw himself into minor activities and run the risk of getting but rarely onto a high spiritual level.[15]

Gordon was of the opinion that the Anglican clergy mainly chose the latter path and became experts in arranging canteens and cinema shows. He believed the answer was in compromise and was also one of perception:

> Those of us who feel pressed by his dilemma are occupying much of our time with those things the soldiers would describe as non-religious, but on every opportunity we are preaching consistently and insistently the all-inclusiveness of Christianity. Christianity in terms of ordinary duty.[16]

He concludes "and we are learning a truer sympathy which may fit us better in the coming days to supply deeper needs."[17]

The dilemma facing chaplains was addressed by the Revd Harry Blackburne, Assistant Chaplain General, in his booklet *Advice to Chaplains*. Under the heading 'Social Work' he says:

> You should try and take as many opportunities as possible of organising and associating yourselves with social work for the benefit of both officers and men, remembering always that you must not let it interfere with your spiritual work by taking up too much of your time and energy.[18]

He realises that this attitude will be of help with the spiritual nature of the chaplains' job.

> You will find it a great opportunity of making many close friendships. You will find that those who have seen you active on their behalf during the week on behalf of their material welfare will listen to you all the more readily on Sundays and will come to you constantly for help advice and comfort.[19]

The epitome of this necessity to meld spiritual with physical and material support was perhaps best found in the activities of the Revd Phillip 'Tubby' Clayton at Talbot House in Poperinghe. The idea of a house for rest and recreation for all, men and officers, was the brainchild of Neville Talbot in memory of his brother Gilbert who had died at

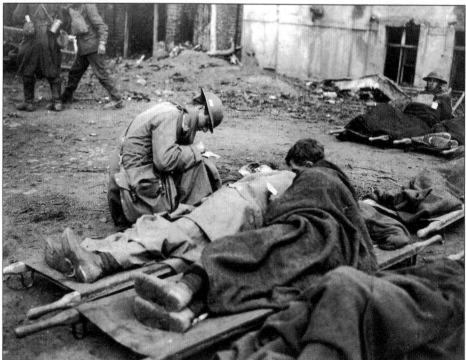

A chaplain writing a postcard for a wounded man, Noyelles. (IWM Q9518)

The Revd G. A. Studdert Kennedy, 'Woodbine Willie' (RAChD Archives)

Sanctuary Wood in July 1915. The house at Poperinghe has been described as a 'Haven in Hell.' Here the troops could find facilities such as the library, a piano, writing equipment and also relax in the garden. The house had a policy of equality between ranks and Tubby had a sign over his study door, 'Abandon rank all ye who enter here'. Thousands of troops passed through the doors during the war and it became the place to leave messages for friends and colleagues who had lost touch with one other. As well as the recreational side the house had a beautiful chapel in the roof eaves where a constant stream of services took place. Here privates and generals went to talk to God in the peaceful loft. Here many took their first and some their last communion. Order was kept by Tubby in a good-natured way, by a series of humorous and sometime sarcastic notices, 'signal phial please', and 'if you have been used to spitting on the carpet at home, please spit here.' Tubby had the gift of friendship to all types and conditions of men and his gifts ranged from being an expert scrounger to a confidante and counsellor. The sort of atmosphere engendered by Tubby in Talbot House is an example of the way in which good chaplains could minister to the physical and spiritual needs of the soldier while maintaining an independence from military rank and authority.

Louden has come to the conclusion that in the chaplains' writings "Religion is either taken for granted or appears only incidentally."[20] It can be seen from the extracts from chaplains mentioned above that a great deal of thought was given by many chaplains to the problem of reconciling the demands made on them. The demands made by the army, and to some extent their own sense of Christian duty, to supply material needs conflicted with their desire to concentrate on the more spiritual aspects of their calling as chaplains. In the organisational limbo that, particularly in the early days of the war, characterised their role, they strove to bring the love and reality of God to the men under their care. If many decided that was best done by being close to the men in their every day concerns of where the next cigarette or meal was coming from then who can categorically say they were wholly wrong? Studdert Kennedy captures the uncertainty but resolution present in the chaplain's role in his famous encounter with the Revd Theodore Bayley Hardy:

> He (Bayley Hardy) asked me about purely spiritual works. I said there is very little; it is all muddled and mixed. Take a box of fags in your haversack and a great deal of love in your heart and go up with them. You can pray with them sometimes but pray for them always.[21]

Studdert Kennedy grew to dislike his nickname and in his poem 'Woodbine Willie' ruefully comments "For the men to whom I owed God's peace I put off with a cigarette".[22]

This comment shows the constant heart searching that Studdert Kennedy and many chaplains did concerning the 'chaplain's dilemma.' The 'chaplain's dilemma' in terms of the rights or wrongs of 'holy grocery' is still present both in the army and in the parish. There will always be discussion about the pros and cons of spiritual or active pastoral care. The Scottish padre Lachlan Watt seems to sum up the dilemma of the First World War chaplain thus: "A chaplain's life is not, as so many think, a thing of services. It is rather a thing of service."[23]

Notes.

1.   G. Gordon and T. Pym, *Papers from Picardy*, p. 107.
2.   Stephen Louden, *Chaplains in Conflict*, p. 43.
3.   The Revd Duncan Blair, 'Leaves from the Journal of a Scottish Padre in the First World War', *Royal Army Chaplains' Department Quarterly Journal* Vol 18, June 1954, pp 44-50.
4.   Louden, op. cit., p. 45.
5.   Ibid, p. 46.
6.   F. R. Barry, *Period of My Life*, p. 60.
7.   Ibid, p. 61.
8.   Jonathan Horne, (ed), *The Best of Good Fellows*, p. 154.
9.   John Bickersteth, (ed), *The Bickersteth Diaries*, p. 84.
10.   Ibid, p. 75.
11.   Stuart John Maclaren, (ed), *Somewhere in Flanders*, p. 15.
12.   Lachlan Maclean Watt, *In France and Flanders with the Fighting Men*, p. viii.
13.   Revd Horsley Smith, 'A Chaplain's Recollections of 1917-1918', *Royal Army Chaplains' Department Quarterly Journal* Vol 24, December 1978, pp 19-25.
14.   Gordon and Pym, op. cit., p. 110.
15.   Ibid, p. 108.
16.   Ibid, p. 112.
17.   Ibid, p. 115.
18.   H. Blackburne, Letters and papers from the R.A.Ch.D. Archives.
19.   Ibid.
20.   Louden, op. cit., p. 53.
21.   J.K. Mozley et al., *G.A. Studdert Kennedy by his Friends*, p. 141.
22.   G. Studdert-Kennedy, poem, 'Woodbine Willie', quoted by A.Wilkinson, op. cit., p. 136.
23.   Lachlan Maclean Watt, op. cit., p. viii.

Chapter 7

Chaplains and the Army

Much of the evidence about the role of chaplain has been taken from the accounts of chaplains themselves. In order to see the significance of their work from the view point of the army it is necessary to examine the relationship that they had with generals, officers and other ranks during the course of their duties.

There is no doubt that many of the highest commanders in the British Army were genuinely and seriously religious and that this piety influenced their conduct in running the war. General Haig was a devout Presbyterian and was influenced in his opinion of the worth of chaplains by his personal chaplain the Revd G.S. Duncan. Haig often visited the Army Chaplains' School at St Omer and kept in close touch with Bishop Gwynne. Haig told Gwynne that his job was the most important under his command.[1] Bishop Gwynne in his diaries frequently recounts occasions when army generals had addressed a group of chaplains at the school. On 8 May 1917 he writes:

> General Jacob of the 2nd Army Corps addressed our chaplains at the school tonight. He gave a very good address full of hints asking the chaplains to identify themselves with the men and not be afraid of the officers.[2]

Chaplain decorating an altar, preparing for a service. (IWM Q11041)

On 16 September General Hobbs addressed the chaplains on 'The duties of the chaplain from an army point of view'.[3] Gwynne remarked in his papers that Generals Horne, Plummer, Byng, Rawlinson and Gough were remarkable for the earnestness of their religious faith. Generals Horne, Gough and Allenby were very supportive of the national mission at the front. Lord Cavan famously attributed his successful role as commander to periods of prayer in the upper room at Talbot House.[4]

It would seem that there was a strong mutual regard and cooperation between senior commanders of the army and the Army Chaplains' Department that helped them work well together. This relationship has been the source of yet more criticism of the army chaplain in the First World War. This asserts that the chaplains were used by the High Command as morale boosters of a very important kind and that they showed displays of bellicosity in boosting this morale that were wholly inappropriate for their calling. The accusation is that, in their more spiritual and pastoral roles, they encouraged the 'fighting spirit' of the troops by sermons and talks and that their contribution to raising military morale became the chief value in the eyes of the generals and high command.

Michael Snape thinks that the relaxation of the order forbidding chaplains from the front was the result of a growing realisation by commanders that the chaplains could be useful morale boosters in a military sense as well as a material one. Snape defines morale thus "The overall willingness of individual units and the soldiers which comprise them to endure manifold hazards and discomforts of war."[5] It is his opinion that it was the realisation of the chaplains' potential use in this respect that was a major reason for the relaxation of restrictions on chaplains' movements.

The Conference of Army Commanders at Cassel held on 15 January 1916 was an important part of this process of enabling chaplains to find a role for themselves on the front line. The BEF's Adjutant General confirmed that restrictions on the movement of chaplains were lifted.

Church Parade, Basra. (RAChD Archives)

It is important to look at the background of both the chaplains and the army in the context of early 20th Century Britain. The Anglican Church had been a significant part of the culture of Edwardian Britain and the concept of 'Muscular Christianity'. In the slum parishes of most industrial cities the church had started military-style youth organisations and there was also the Church Army. Many of the soldiers in the front line would have attended Sunday School and been exposed to the simpler elements of the Christian faith. Many of the officers would have been products of the public schools that emphasised the importance of religious observance. Many of Kitchener's volunteer army would have been churchgoers. It was therefore natural that Anglican Chaplains would have had a certain amount of authority and credibility with the men and officers of the British army. It was perhaps inevitable that their role would have developed from a much undefined one in the first 18 months of the war into one that the High Command could see as vital for the raising and maintaining of morale.

The Generals had a good deal to do with this perception of chaplains as morale keepers. Haig is quoted often as an admirer of chaplains. "A good chaplain is as valuable as a good general" he says when speaking to the Senior Chaplain of the First Army, the Revd Harry Blackburne in early 1917.[6] Stephen Louden in his discussion on chaplains and morale says of this quote "An observation both flattering and ambiguous."[7] Louden uses several quotes from generals to put his point that the chaplains were merely mouthpieces of morale boosting propaganda. An example is a quotation from a letter from Haig to Gwynne in August 1916. "My dear bishop … that the troops are in such splendid heart and morale is largely attributable to our chaplains who have successfully made our men realise what we are fighting for and for the justice of our cause."[8]

The memoirs of the Revd E C Crosse bring out the ambivalence of the chaplains to their perceived role by High Command as morale boosters. He talks a lot about morale and the role of chaplains in maintaining it but it is questionable whether this morale is the same sort as discussed at the Cassel conference. His attitude is that the soldiers were, of necessity, at war and that the role for the chaplain was to sustain them spiritually through their experience. He realises that the ordinary soldier is not very bellicose. "In his attitude to the enemy the British soldier displayed both charity and common sense … lectures on the subject that the only kind of German is a dead one don't usually cut much ice."[9]

He has quite trenchant views on the value of church parades as military rather than a purely religious occasion. "The Chaplain who knew his duty could accomplish much on these occasions not in the way of teaching the mysteries of religion but by improving the general morale."[10] He seems to have taken the parade service as an opportunity of showing how useful chaplains could be and thereby improving their credibility and standing, but he is very aware that this is not their primary purpose:

> All forms of discipline are useless except in so far as they encourage an inner discipline, which is not dependant on inspection, and religion is beyond question the most effective way of implanting this inner spirit.[11]

Is this the sort of attitude that the generals are talking about when they are praising the chaplains for raising morale? If so, it is very different to the idea that they were instilling bellicosity and fighting spirit by glorifying war under a religious banner. Crosse realises that the increase in the chaplain's influence arose from the perception that they were now serving some useful purpose. "Once the supervision of morale was extended to cover the supervision of morals, there was no longer any possibility of the padres' job being regarded as a sinecure.[12]

But he is very aware of the distinctions between his definition of morale and the possible interpretation of the generals. He considers that there are two very different aspects of morale. The 'fighting spirit' needed for battles and the 'spirit of endurance' needed to survive life in the trenches. If chaplains could provide help and comfort to men in the name of God, then they were carrying out their pastoral responsibilities, no matter what the generals thought that were doing. Crosse also explained that, though chaplains became increasingly welcome in the trenches for military reasons, the religious and pastoral were uppermost in the minds of the chaplains. "Conversation on these occasions turned … very rarely on the realities of war. There was more peace talk to be heard in the line itself than anywhere and it would have been foolish to stop it."[13]

Although the close cooperation between the army commanders and the Army Chaplains Department has been criticised in terms of the chaplains' role in the war, it cannot be denied that the generals were motivated by religious feelings as well as military considerations. The attributes required from men fighting a war such as that in the trenches of the First World War were, after all, in some ways the same as living a religious life i.e. trusting in God, self-sacrifice, selflessness, a sense of giving oneself for a higher cause. General Horne sums up this attitude in a letter supporting the national mission.

> History tells us how men fight for a cause which concerns their religion. If we have religious enthusiasm, with a high standard of devotion to duty and self sacrifice which inspires our troops we gain a great deal.[14]

The attitude of officers and men to chaplains is more difficult to determine. Officers' accounts of their war are useful but often critical. Those published depend on material likely to appeal to an audience in the late 1920s and 1930s who were disillusioned by the war and ready for any type of criticism of the way the war was handled, let alone that of chaplains. Robert Graves, Siegfried Sassoon, Guy Chapman and C E Montague were well-known literary figures that were scathing of the chaplains' performance in the war. However, their criticism stands and can give us a good idea of the problems faced by chaplains in their public image. Graves' main criticism of the chaplains rested on the contrast between them and the Roman Catholic priests who were allowed to go the front line from the beginning of the war. He said of the Anglican Chaplains "Soldiers could hardly respect a chaplain who obeyed these orders, yet not one in fifty seem sorry to obey them."[15] Guy Chapman also used this comparison, "The Church of Rome sent me into battle mentally and spiritually cleaned. The Church of England could only offer you a cigarette."[16] As we have seen with is opinions of chaplains in ambulances, Graves often argued from the particular to the general and was often wide of the mark, whereas Schweitzer believes that many British officers did not share Graves' views and claims that his doubts about the bible "Got on his fellow officers nerves."[17]

Ostensibly officers would have much in common with the chaplain as they came on the whole from the same social class and shared similar values. The Bishop of Kensington, writing to the father of an officer who had died, comments on the many Anglican laymen who had been working in boys' slum clubs and university East End missions in the years before the war. "I have often thought how wonderfully God was preparing those boys at the university by that mission for the great service which they were being called."[18] Other examples of committed Anglican laymen were Burgon Bickersteth, Bernard Adams and

Donald Hankey. According to Richard Holmes one tenth of army officers in 1910 were sons of clergy.[19] However, as we have seen, during the first year of the war the chaplains were experiencing ideological and practical difficulties. The original instructions about their place in battle caused resentment and sometimes ridicule from officers, as did the fact that they were allowed to return home if they wished after their year's contract. In the chapter about February 1917, one of the contributors to *The War the Infantry Knew*, points out the bad preaching and hypocrisy of one chaplain. The sermon was very jingoistic and he quotes "A man's attitude to war service is quite a simple affair. If he's for it he's for it and vice versa" and comments of the chaplain, "he has vice versa'd back to base already."[20] Many of the thinking officers struggled with the difference between the basic tenants of Christianity and the experience of mass warfare and it was often the chaplains who bore the brunt of this contradiction by being the objects of criticism. In a letter home in December 1917 Corporal Houghton comments on the way his padre had prayers about "Not leading us into any kind of danger" and continues,

> I am quite sure the chaplain has never noticed the inconsistency of that phrase any more than the clergymen out here who profess a religion that teaches us that all men should be brothers and yet pray weekly for victory over our enemies.[21]

Some officers were hostile to chaplains and did their best to thwart arrangements for services. Hood recounts a conversation with Hetherington, commanding officer in Nov 1915 in Gallipoli.

> H: I don't know if you will have many men at your service.
> Self: Why colonel, you made the arrangements yourself.
> H: Yes, but I've a more important job, the men are digging out the latrines.[22]

Several officers in their memoirs have good things to say about the chaplains they experienced. Victor Richardson, correspondent and friend of Vera Brittain, was impressed with his padre "A very fine preacher ... the padre takes the most practical view of the

United Parade Service, Bethune, Sunday 6th April 1916. (IWM 54987)

Trinity."[23] Geoffrey King, an officer in the Machine Gun Corps, was impressed by his chaplain – "It is extraordinary how I have got to admire – I had almost written love – that man."[24] Close bonds often grew between chaplains attached to field ambulances and their officers. Letters of condolence to Zoë Doudney, widow of the Revd Charles Doudney, show how he had been admired and his friendship valued. Lt John Annan of Field Hospital No. 8 near Ypres writes from "One who admired our padre much."[25] His colleagues at the 18th Ambulance wrote "We voice the regret of the whole ambulance on losing a much loved padre."[26] The Revd D. Winifrith, who spent several years attached to an ambulance, talks of the deep friendships developed with officers of the ambulance. The Revd Guy Rogers, working with the Guards Brigades in France, although finding relations with officers difficult at first, worked hard at winning the confidence of the officers he messed with. In February 1915 he writes "Great discussion at lunch. They push me on now to discuss all sorts of religious and philosophical questions … It is pleasant to feel one's position is assured and gives me confidence to try and get further."[27]

The attitude of men in the ranks to chaplains is harder to ascertain. Books such as Frank Richards' *Old Soldiers Never Die* contained much that was critical of chaplains and the novel *Retreat* by R E Benstead paints a picture of a padre with very little idea of his role in the army. Memoirs of rankers are scarcer than those of officers and generals and do not often contain lengthy observations of the role of the chaplain.

Chaplains were at a disadvantage in their attempts to get close to the men by their rank and position in the army. Although they were conscious of the fact that they needed to be where the men were, and put much emphasis on visiting in both base camp and in the trenches, they did, in reality, live with the officers. Stephen Graham in *Private in the Guards* comments on the perception that the chaplains were more ideologically attuned to the officers' point of view:

> What struck me most about them was the extraordinary way they seemed to make their minds fit to the official demands made upon opinion: they always rapidly absorbed the official point of view about the war and often the officers' point of view as well.[28]

He continues:

> Officers lived at ease and whereas the men had poor food they ate and drank in the company of officers – I could not help feeling how badly handicapped the padres were."[29]

It has been suggested that chaplains were hampered by their social class and their inability to relate to working class men *en masse*. It must be remembered, however, that many of these chaplains had worked in big cities and slum parishes. Many had worked 'missions' in the East End as students and also run clubs for men in their parishes. It was the expectation in parishes before the war that every house was visited regularly. Chaplains were probably more in tune with working class life that many of the officers. The job of chaplains in censoring letters often revealed to them the opinions of the men on matters of religion. Richard Holmes is of the opinion that this "enabled them to see, as a modern researcher can, just how deep a current of belief flowed through the army."[30]

As with the officers, there was resentment that initially the padres were kept back. Church parades also caused resentment and they did not endear the chaplain to the

Sentry: Halt ! Who goes there ?
Voice: "Army Chaplain"
Sentry: "Pass Charlie Chaplin—
                        All's well ! "

A First World War cartoon of an Army Chaplain. (Author's collection)

ordinary soldier. Frank Richards commented "If we happened to be out of the line on a Sunday we had church parade which 95% of the men detested."[31] Although senior chaplains like Harry Blackburne issued orders concerning breaking up the formality of the services, not using a 'parsonical' voice and keeping the sermon short and to the point, they do not seem to have been very popular, and as we have seen, many chaplains stopped having them and concentrated on voluntary services instead. They did however, link religion with army discipline to the detriment of the chaplains' popularity.

The recent publication of books such as *Forgotten Voices* using the archives of the Imperial War Museum has provided some more evidence on the attitude of soldiers to chaplains.

Sergeant W Daniels of the Royal Artillery:

My first experience in the trenches concerned the padre ... he arrived from Brigade HQ and I was pleased to see a man of that description risking his life coming to the front line trenches. He asked me how I felt in regard to God and was I frightened? I said I was frightened, more than once. "Would you like me to pray, or would you like to pray with me?" He then asked. I said I'd very much like to, and we knelt on the fire step ... and prayed there.[32]

Private Norman Demuth of the London Regiment sheds light on the role and difficulties of the padre visiting the front line trenches. "From the practical point of view, there was no religion in the front line, although our unit padre used to come and visit us quite a lot. But he was never allowed to stay in one place too long because he got in the way." He goes on to comment on how the work of the padres behind the line was also appreciated.

When we were on rest our padre would come round to the billets – ours was very good indeed. And when I was wounded and got to hospital I thanked heaven for the padres, they were wonderful. They came around and took down your name and address and wrote your casualty postcard and generally looked after you. They never ranted, they never told you what a sinner you were … and if they said a prayer it was a short one.[33]

As many chaplains realised quite early in the war, the respect they received from the troops was directly related to the courage shown by the padres in action. Chaplains like Studdert Kennedy and Bayley Hardy became famous for their attitude of staying with the men in battle. No doubt they did much to raise the profile of chaplains in the eyes of the ordinary soldier, but the Army Book of Archbishop Gwynne in which he recorded details of the chaplains and saved press cuttings of reports of many brave actions by padres, shows that their attitude and action were not atypical of the chaplains generally. When soldiers realised this they were pleased and grateful. Corporal Clifford of the Hertfordshire Regiment:

We were told that we'd got to get to a stream called Steenbeeck. We got there and were told to lie down prone. We were all lying when suddenly I felt an object fall at my side. I looked around and it was a tin of woodbines. I looked again and there was a padre. I'd never seen a padre take part in an attack, and whoever he was he was worthy of the highest praise, because he was in a very dangerous position.[34]

Although chaplains fitted in well for the most part with the officers and had much in common with them they had difficulties in convincing many of them of the relevance of their specifically religious role at the front, as opposed to their usefulness as an organiser of recreation and an extra man in the dressing station in battle. It was up to the individual chaplain to seize moments in messes and trenches to talk about spiritual matters. Schweitzer has stated that the subalterns as a whole held on to their Christian faith[35] and this must reflect to some extent a rapport with the chaplains at the front.

The relationships of chaplains with the other ranks were fraught from the beginning with class tension and anti-clericalism, which was a hangover from the pre-war years. However, many chaplains found that by seeking out their flock, especially sharing their difficulties and dangers in the front line that they could win their respect and achieve a deeper relationship.

Notes

1. H.C. Jackson, *Pastor on the Nile*, p.164.
2. The diaries and papers of Bishop Llewellyn Henry Gwynne (XACC/18/Z/1, XACC/18/F/1).
3. Ibid.
4. T. Lever, *Clayton of Toc H*, p.61.
5. Michael Snape, *God and the British Soldier*, p.91.
6. H. Blackburne, *This Also Happened*, p.115.
7. S. Louden, *Chaplains in Conflict*, p.47.
8. Ibid, p.48.
9. E.C. Crosse Papers, IWM (80/22/1)
10. Crosse, p.24
11. Crosse, p.23
12. Crosse, p.51
13. Crosse, p.57
14. General Horne, 'An address to the Chaplains, 1st Corps, 06/03/16', Archives of the RAChD.
15. Robert Graves, *Goodbye to All That*, p.158.
16. Guy Chapman, *A Passionate Prodigality*, p.117.
17. Richard Schweizter, *The Cross and the Trenches*, p.85.
18. Mervyn Evers papers IWM (78/7/1)
19. Richard Holmes, *Tommy*, p.506.
20. J.C. Dunn, *The War the Infantry Knew*, p.94.
21. Malcolm Brown, *1918 Year of Victory*, p.13.
22. C.I.S. Hood Papers, IWM (90/7/1)
23. Letter from Victor Richardson to Vera Brittain, Schweitzer, op. cit., p.171.
24. Ibid.
25. Jonathan Horne, ed, *The Best of Good Fellows*, p.186.
26. Ibid, p.182.
27. T. G. Rogers, papers, IWM (7/107/1).
28. Stephen Graham, *Private in the Guards*, pp256-7.
29. Ibid., p. 253.
30. Holmes, op.cit., p.552.
31. Frank Richards, *Old Soldiers Never Die*, p.84.
32. Max Arthur, *Forgotten Voices*, p.138.
33. Ibid, p.165.
34. Ibid, p.221.
35. Schweitzer, op. cit., p.85.

Chapter 8

Religion and the Army

At the outbreak of war there was a hopeful feeling among the churches that there would be a revival of religion amongst the officers and men of the British Army. Donald Hankey commented on contemporary opinions on the 'churches opportunity,'[1] Wilkinson says that "Some at home in the early days of the war, hearing the stories of hymn singing … Eucharists in barns … concluded that at the front a religious revival was underway."[2] The visit by the Bishop of London to the Western Front in April 1915 was widely reported and his views of the religious feeling among the troops put a very positive slant on the health of religion at the front. An officer who was detailed to accompany the bishops wrote in a report for *The Times* on 12 April:

> All along the line from start to finish everyone, from generals commanding to the lowest ranks, showed clearly that the sense of spiritual things animates strongly all grades of the British Army in the field.[3]

The Bishop commented in an article published in *The Times*,

> The truth of the matter is that the realities of war have melted away the surface shyness of men about religion. They feel that they are up against questions of life and death. I have met more than one censor who, for the first time, has realised the part religion bears in a soldier's life by censoring the innumerable letters home in which the writers ask for the prayers of the peoples at home or express their trust in God.[4]

Kitchener's army, both officers and men, had come from religious backgrounds. Many ordinands and clergy served in the RAMC and the ranks. A high proportion of officers were committed Anglican laymen, like Donald Hankey, or sons of the clergy, like Burgon Bickersteth or both. Michael Snape considers that "The presence of a leavening (and in substantial pockets) of pre-war churchgoers among the men of the British Army in the first two years of the war did much to explain the strong impression that many churchmen had of a religious revival in the British Army at the time."[5] Many accounts of chaplains recall occasions on which they felt that a wave of religious feeling was present in their encounters with the men. An example is the Revd Hood's account of his experiences in Gallipoli:

> A wonderful spirit has come over the men. Men have learned to pray – the old habit has come back and in the billet that all might know, there are those who kneel down and commune with their God and Saviour.[6]

A nurse, writing to *The Times*, says

Everywhere over there one is astounded and uplifted by the reverent perception of our fighting men of the spiritual values which are as necessary as the material ones to the conduct of war.[7]

Notwithstanding this leavening, and the many tales of piety and religious feeling at the front from individual chaplains, many contemporary observers and chaplains had a pessimistic view of the depth of religious feeling at the front. The Revd Tom Pym pointed out that although under abnormal conditions people will often turn to religion, when they become accustomed to the new situation the concern for religion declines. The Revd F R Barry in his paper 'Faith in the light of war' observed, "It is untrue ... that war is a reviver of religion."[8] He goes on to deny that there has been a revival but continues "it is something no one has seen ... if it did it would be most suspicious, an extremely dangerous exotic growth, for war is a spiritual narcotic."[9] There he put his finger on the essential dilemma of the chaplain at the front. On the one hand they are looking for an increasing devotion and church attendance from the soldiers and officers, but when these appear they often distrust them as religious feeling brought on by 'Wind up religion'.

However, chaplains such as Neville Talbot realised that the gauging of the religious feelings of the men was a complicated business. He would not call 'Wind up' religion cowardice as did Studdert Kennedy at times, but neither would he call it Christian. He says in his *Thoughts on religion at the front* "A good many which are current at home about religion at the front are a good distance removed from reality."[10]

F R Barry concludes that there is a considerable amount of 'true religion' that he considers to be perhaps nearer the real thing than what the pre-war church would call 'religious'. He believes that "Men's conduct and their outlook are to a large extent unconsciously Christian", but adds "their creed is most emphatically not."[11] Neville Talbot pursued this theme of the way in which inarticulate religion was expressed. "Deep in their hearts is a great trust and faith in God. It is an inarticulate faith expressed in deeds."[12] This opinion is echoed by Michael Snape – "Contemporary churchmen were probably too disposed to take a pessimistic view of the religious condition of British Society and of the British soldiers in particular."[13]

Many wartime chaplains commented on the apparent ignorance of both men and officers in theology and doctrine. They bemoan the fact that Sunday school and state education have proved so inadequate in equipping the ordinary Englishman with the intellectual and theological weapons to help in time of total war. Therefore, says Neville Talbot, "There is a great heart in the people. It is not a great mind. ... There is not on the whole a great articulate revival of the Christian religion at the front."[14] Donald Hankey in his article 'The Religion of the Inarticulate' goes further. He believes that the ordinary soldiers did believe in "unselfishness, generosity, charity and humility, but it is doubtful whether they connected these qualities with the profession and practice of Christianity."[15] He considers that the average soldier thought that Christianity meant "...setting yourself up to be better than your neighbours, no drinking, no swearing and probably no smoking."[16] The Revd Mervyn Evers tried to combat the fatalism so often shown by the men. "By and large their philosophy was very much that you were all right until the bullet with your regimental number came up along and then your number was up."[17] He tried to share with them his own philosophy "to commit oneself wholly to Christ so that it was his responsibility to see whether you lived or died."[18]

The report 'The Army and Religion' grew out of conversations of D S Cairns, Professor of the United Free College at Aberdeen, while he was at a base camp in Rouen.

Comments by Neville Talbot and his conversations with chaplains and soldiers convinced him of the need to find out the nature of faith in the army. He writes in his introduction to the report about the necessity to the church to know about the religious feeling at the front. "It is of vital importance that they should know what faiths and what ideals these men are living by, and what change if any the war is creating in their souls."[19]

A committee was set up representing all the churches under the chairmanship of Bishop Talbot and financed by the YMCA. The research began in 1917 and the authors received over 3,000 replies to their questions. Three questions were asked.

1. What did men think about religion, morality and society?
2. Had the war made men more open to religious appeal or had it created new difficulties for belief?
3. What proportion of men were vitally connected to the churches and what did they think of the churches?

Many of the replies were of the same tenor as the statement attributed to Neville Talbot "The soldier has got religion; I am not so sure that he has got Christianity."[20] A Presbyterian Chaplain replied "As a whole they are religious but not Christian, the men as a whole are not hostile to church religion, but are rather indifferent."[21] There was respect for Jesus in that men often revered him as a fellow sufferer, "it is the crucified Christ rather than the risen Christ that appeals."[22] There seemed to be little concept of the incarnation and atonement. Much discussion on the problems of pain and suffering and the triumph of evil or good was reported and a "fair amount of serious thought about what happens when we die."[23] The opinion seemed to be that all the best instincts feel that man will get a fair judgment and chances of improvement in another world. [24]

There were conflicting opinions on the way in which the war had changed soldiers. A chaplain in the Scottish Regiment found that "A great many men have a sense of God's presence with them and pray to him with a firm belief that he is concerned with individuals' lives, and able to protect." However, he goes on to say that "a very large number of men have found new difficulties for faith as a result of war. With some it has resulted in complete loss of faith in a personal God."[25]

Wilkinson describes how the war produced many troubling paradoxes for Christians who believed that people were either good or bad or that good deeds could only be done by the consciously accepted grace of god. "The war produced heroism and comradeship but also encouraged swearing, drunkenness, dishonesty gambling and impurity."[26]

The report continued by explaining that although men often believed in God, respected Jesus and thought a lot about the concept of good and evil, and that their behaviour in battle threw up the qualities that we associate with Christianity, that the men themselves did not associate these qualities with Christianity. They considered Christianity to be a negative set of ideas and as something irrelevant to their lives. In Chapter 4 of the report, titled 'Misunderstandings', a chaplain of experience said, "Institutional religion was widely identified with respectability and a negative code, but a generous or unselfish act was called "Really Christian."[27]

The report goes on to consider the reasons for the very mixed and in some places depressing picture of religious life at the front. The social and economic background to life in post-Industrial Revolution Britain was blamed for a spirit of materialism in the men at the front. In Chapter 5 it is said, "The men take a materialistic, not a spiritual view of life. They have been brought up in a materialistic society."[28] This attitude is blamed on education and the general ignorance of men about religion and doctrine. A female worker blames the Sunday school teachers while a senior chaplain believes that it is not only among working men that this ignorance is found – "The crude religious ideas experienced in officers messes are generally lamentable."[29]

So where does the work of the chaplains fit into this depressing picture painted by the report? We have seen how individual chaplains were encouraged by the reactions of their flock to services, their willingness to be confirmed and their thoughtfulness in discussion, but were still painfully aware that the majority of soldiers were untouched by formal Christianity. Donald Hankey describes how chaplains pondering on their 'Great Opportunity' asked:

> Did it mean that there was an opportunity of providing soldiers with free note paper and supplies? – If so they agreed. There was an opportunity and that the church had risen to the occasion. But if it meant that there was an opportunity of bringing the erring back to the fold they wished that someone would come and show them how it ought to be done.[30]

Officers and men had difficulty reconciling war with the Christian faith. Christopher Stone, an officer in the 22nd Royal Fusiliers, wrote home to his wife, "I have argued with the chaplain out here about Christianity and the war and maintained the war is *not* Christianity's chance at all … it is opposed to war and no juggling of texts make it approve of war."[31]

Hankey believed that the opportunity to associate the values of unselfishness, generosity and charity with Christianity were lost, as what was associated with Christianity was "A smug self-righteousness which Christ spent all his life trying to destroy."[32] He claims that it was a failure on the part of chaplains not to recognise that the inarticulateness of the soldier did not mean that he lacked religion. "I am certain that if the chaplain wants to be understood and win their sympathy he must begin by showing that Christianity is the explanation and justification and the triumph of all they do now really believe in."[33] The criticisms of Hankey are of a different nature than those of Graves, Sasoon et al, as he is considering the difficulties they are working under, but is urging them to make the most of the pastoral opportunities given to them in time of war.

So why was there no revival in the trenches? Schweitzer attributes the lack of a religious revival in the trenches to the resentment caused by what soldiers saw as the acceptance of the nationalist cause by Anglican chaplains linked with their initial difficulties in being present in the front line. C E Montague, a journalist who joined up in his forties, said in his 1922 book, *Disenchantment* that the chaplains had lost an opportunity of fanning the flame of religious experience. They had failed to bring soldiers across the "The uncrossed threshold of religion."[34] Major John Baynes in his study of the 2nd Scottish Rifles at Neuve Chapelle recounts a soldier seeing a chaplain at the front line, digging a cover for him. Baynes reflects "What a religious revival would have been possible if the chaplains had shared the dangers of the trenches."[35]

Richard Schweitzer sees this view as too simplistic. He points out that the American chaplains also failed to produce a revival despite not experiencing the difficulties of the Anglican chaplain and the inbuilt anti-clericalism of the British soldier. He considered that the upbringing and university education of chaplains and the institutional nature of the army worked against an emotional outpouring of religion in the trenches.

Neville Talbot blames the absence of a religious revival both on the nature of total war and the lack of spiritual equipment and education to deal with it. He admitted that to too many soldiers it appeared that "Godwards there sometimes seems to be a great darkness"[36] and that to men in the trenches religion seemed not to offer "the slightest relief". He thought that "War being what it is, the absence of a religious revival during it is not surprising", and blamed this partially on the state of the church and religious education before the war. "We have been overtaken by the cataclysm of war in a condition of great poverty towards God."[37] The report called 'The Army and Religion' when discussing the 'Moral impact of war' is of the opinion that the dehumanising effects of war were not conducive to religious thinking: "Those that are able to reduce themselves most nearly to the machine survive in comparative comfort."[38] Several references are made to soldiers 'not thinking, simply carrying on."[39]

Another contemporary observer, news reporter Phillip Gibbs, agrees with this idea that the sheer awfulness of war outweighed the attempts of the chaplains to preach a God of love.

> The devotion of military chaplains to the wounded, their valour, their decorations for gallantry under fire, their human comradeship, and spiritual sincerity, would not bridge the gulf in the minds of many soldiers, between a gospel of love and this argument by bayonet and bomb, gas shell and high velocity, blunderbuss club and trench shovel.[40]

In his study of the army and religion in the two World Wars, Michael Snape used the term 'diffusive Christianity' which churchmen had started using in the early 20th Century to paint, in some ways, a more positive picture of the religious nature of the men fighting in the trenches. He describes it as a "non dogmatic form of Christianity, one which derived its currency from a sense of religion's social utility and from an almost universal (if generally limited) measure of religious education."[41] This manifested itself throughout society, from the upper classes support of established religion to the working man understanding of religion as a moral code rather than a regime of attendance at church. Snape argued that this 'diffusive Christianity' was widespread and shown in the trenches by fatalism, dependence on mascots and amulets, reverence of calvaries, but often evidenced by more conventional desire for religious services and prayers. Churchmen, he believed were "too readily inclined to dismiss symptoms of more orthodox religiosity among soldiers as worthless manifestations of emergency religion."[42]

The chaplains then had many issues militating against their work of preaching the gospel and expanding religious awareness at the front. Unrealistic expectations from church leaders and civilians at home who were expecting religious revival led to disillusionment and heart-searching by the chaplains at the front. What Snape describes as the inoculating effect of diffusive Christianity prevented many men from going further in exploring the Christian faith and when the realities of war hit home, the religious instruction provide by the Sunday and Church schools proved inadequate to sustain faith in difficult situations. The report 'The Army and Religion' confirmed what chaplains such as Neville Talbot and committed laymen such as Donald Hankey already knew, that religion, where it existed, was often inarticulate, God-centred but not specifically Christian. It was often simple, consisting of the practice of Christian virtues and fatalism. There seems to be a contrast between the accounts of individual chaplains who were often enthusiastic and positive about their work and the institutional pessimism of the Report on the Army and Religion. The report placed much emphasis on the failings of the church before the war and was full of ideas about what should be done after the war.

For most of the chaplains at the front line life was concentrated on the daily routine and on doing the best they could.

Notes

1. Donald Hankey, *A Student in Arms,* p.101.
2. Alan Wilkinson, *The Church of England in the First World War,* p.159.
3. *The Times,* 12 April 1915.
4. *The Times,* 13 April 1915.
5. Michael Snape, *God and the British Soldier,* p.164.
6. C.I.O. Hood Papers, IWM (90/7/1).
7. Annie Swann, Letter to *The Times,* 14 October 1915.
8. F. Barry, 'Faith in the Light of War', article in The Revd B. Macnutt (ed), *The Church in the Furnace,* p.35.
9. bid, p.52.
10. Neville Talbot, *Thoughts on Religion at the Front,* p.2.
11. Barry, op. cit., p.54.
12. Talbot, op. cit., p.8.
13. Snape, op. cit., p.57.
14. Talbot, op. cit. p 10-11.
15. Hankey, op. cit., p.110.
16. Ibid, p.112.
17. Mervyn Evers Papers, IWM (78/7/1).
18. Ibid.
19. D. Cairns (ed), *The Army and Religion,* p.xxvi.
20. Ibid, p.9.
21. Ibid, p.34.
22. Ibid, p.42.
23. Ibid, p.18.
24. Ibid, p.18.
25. Ibid, p.26.
26. Wilkinson, op. cit., p.162.
27. Cairns, op. cit., p 70.
28. Ibid, chap. 5.
29. Ibid, p.109.
30. Hankey, op. cit., p.102.
31. Christopher Stone, *A Private in the Guards,* quoted by M. Snape, op. cit., p.113.
32. Hankey, op. cit., p.113.
33. Ibid, p.114.
34. C.E. Montague, *Disenchantment,* quoted by Wilkinson, op. cit., p.118.
35. John Baynes, *Morale,* quoted by Wilkinson, op.cit., p.119.
36. Talbot, op. cit., p.17.
37. Ibid, p.17.
38. Cairns, op. cit., p.84.
39. Ibid, chap 6, also chap 1 p.6.
40. Phillip Gibbs, quoted by Snape, op. cit., p 113.
41. Snape, op. cit., p.22.
42. Ibid, p.58.

Chapter 9

Some Notable Chaplains

The historiography of the First World War contains a sizeable content on the work of the Army Chaplains' Department during the war. There are many contemporary accounts by chaplains, that is perhaps not surprising, given the nature of their education and background. Chaplains figure largely, as we have seen, in the iconoclastic accounts of war produced during the 1930s and have found a place in revisionist historians work in the later 20th Century. Despite the often critical views expressed about their role there can be no doubt that individual chaplains have captured the imagination and earned the respect of the generations since the Great War.

Some, like the Revd Phillip 'Tubby' Clayton, and the Revd Geoffrey Studdert Kennedy ('Woodbine Willie'), became household names due to their widespread reputation with returning troops. Some, like the Revd Noel Mellish VC and the Revd Theodore Bayley Hardy VC, became renowned for their courage in action. Many went on to be the leading churchmen of the 20th Century. There are many that could be described as 'notable chaplains', including chaplains like Julian Bickersteth, who in his contributions to the Bickersteth Family Letters, produced a detailed and spirited account of the life of the chaplain, the Revd Maurice Peel who died going into action with his men at Bullecourt, and the Revd Harry Blackburne who did so much to organise the Army Chaplains Department on the Western Front. The chaplains discussed in this chapter are a small sample of the different ways in which chaplains made their contributions to the war.

The Revd Noel Mellish, VC. (RAChD Archives)

Bishop Llewellyn Harry Gwynne

Bishop L.H. Gwynne, Deputy Chaplain General B.E.F. 1915-1918. (RAChD Archives)

"Of all men, Bishop Gwynne did most to win the war." This was the opinion of Lord Plummer, commander of the Second Army, quoted by Dean Inge in his diary in 1934.[1] Although this quotation has been used to reinforce the view that the Army Chaplains' Department acted as a decisive morale booster to the army on the Western Front, it also shows the great respect given to Bishop Gwynne for the way in which he ran the department and the success he had in moulding the chaplains into an organised and effective body. His appointment in July 1915 eased a potentially explosive organisational tension within the Chaplains' Department over the alleged Low Church bias of The Chaplain General, Bishop Taylor Smith, and the growing concern about the organisation of the department and the lack of chaplains in France. His appointment seems to have been universally welcomed and he set about smoothing he ruffled feathers of Anglo Catholic priests and organising the activities and disposition of chaplains more effectively. The Revd Leighton Green commented "His views were ecumenical and he encouraged and supported chaplains of all denominations."[2]

Gwynne was open to all denominations and traditions and treated everyone the same. Bishop Llewellyn Harry Gwynne had been a chaplain during Kitchener's Nile expedition. He stayed on in the Sudan, becoming, as Barry describes the situation "bishop and uncrowned king."[3] At the outbreak of war he returned to Britain to offer his services as chaplain to the expeditionary force, but at 50 was considered too old. Only after persistent visits to the War Office did he succeed in being appointed as Chaplain 4th Class to the army in France. Once there, his diary entries show an increasing sense of dissatisfaction with the way the Chaplains' Department was being run and that it was not, in his opinion, fulfilling its mission. On 20 January 1915 he recounts talking to the Revd Harry Blackburne, then Senior Chaplain to the First Army: "He was very dissatisfied with the lack of method in administering the army department. So am I."[4]

On 1 February 1915, he writes:

There is something wrong about a system which allows the chaplain to be moved far away from the firing line and his flock. I fear the Chaplains' Department suffers from want of an administrator who knows how to adapt his work to the altered situation.[5]

From July of that year he was given this chance and soon set about organising the work of the senior chaplains. Blackburne comments, not long after his appointment, "The Bishop has a splendid grasp of the situation. He says everything depends on the senior chaplains of divisions and he wants me to help any senior chaplains I run into,"[6] and adds "I just love being with him. He is such a man of God and has such a glorious sense of humour." Gwynne appears to have been a great success almost immediately, universally loved for his pastoral care of the chaplains. Barry said of him: "Many of us, I think, would have gone under … had it not been for the pastoral care and guidance of the great and saintly Bishop Gwynne, father in God to a whole generation of young men."[7]

Gwynne's diary contains many entries describing the walks in the woods he had with many of his chaplains, in which he was able to sort out matters of spiritual morale as well as discussing the war and Chaplains' Departmental policy.

Although Barry describes Gwynne as 'Saintly', he also goes on to describe his other attributes. "I have never know anyone less like a saint in a painted window, a burly man and a Welsh footballer he was every inch masculine, a man's man",[8] and describes how "in practical matters he was shrewd and tough."[9] He was certainly shrewd in his dealings with the generals, many of whom he had known as young subalterns in Egypt and the Sudan. He entertained them at his headquarters and kept up a close relationship with the army chiefs that ensured that the Chaplains' Department became integrated fully on the organisational structure of the army.

Wilkinson recounts how Gwynne got on well with General Haig and soon after his appointment, was summoned to Haig's headquarters and told "A good chaplain is as valuable as a good general. We are fighting for Christ and the freedom of mankind."[10] It has been said, of such remarks, that they show how the Army Chaplains' Department was used by the generals to promote the cause. As Louden puts it, that chaplains had "convinced soldiers of the equivalence of the national cause and the will of God."[11] But it is just as likely that Gwynne skilfully used the admiration and support of the generals to ensure that the chaplains were given every support in the trenches by the army and were thereby encouraged in their specific tasks of ministering spiritually to the men. In an article in the *Royal Army Chaplains' Department Journal* in 1923 he explained his reasoning:

> But those who were really responsible for completing the organisation were the generals in the field. It was they who maintained that if their chaplains were to pull their weight and be a spiritual force as well as a valuable factor in keeping up morale of the fighting men, they must fit in as a piece of the great war machine.[12]

An innovation of Gwynne's that had a large effect on the welfare and morale of the chaplains was the creation of a school for chaplains at St Omer in Jan 1917. These became known as 'The Chaplains' Bombing Schools' and provided a week's retreat combined with discussion, time for reading and spiritual refreshment. It was presided over by The Revd B K Cunningham and proved a lifeline to overstretched and exhausted chaplains. Gwynne took a personal interest in the progress of the school and often visited to take services and give talks.

Although becoming an influential and highly thought of part of the churches' work on the Western Front, Gwynne retained his sense of humour and his personal piety. His diaries contain comments and reflections on his own spiritual life. On 16 June 1916 it was his birthday. He asked God for "a passion for Christ and more faith in him."[13] He was the originator of the joke about the Chaplains' Bombing School and told the story of the troops finding a dugout in the trenches labelled 'The Vicarage' and going on to find the 'bloody vicar'. By the end of the war he was a "Beloved father figure, surrounded by a growing saga of his foibles and idiosyncrasies".[14]

At the end of the war, he could have had the pick of preferment in the Anglican Church, but returned to the Sudan to minister there for another 30 years, including the care of chaplains in Egypt in the Second World War. There is no doubt that he had a profound effect on the organisation and welfare of the army chaplains in the First World War. Barry sums it up "What he did for his chaplains can never be told in words."[15]

Revd W E Drury

The Revd W. E. Drury. (Private collection)

In contrast to the influence and power wielded by Gwynne, the Revd William Drury is an example of an ordinary chaplain who was at the mercy of the vagaries of the Army Chaplains' Department and soldiered on ministering to his men through three fronts and three years of war. After being put off volunteering as an army chaplain at the outbreak of war by rumour that there was a long waiting list and by health worries, Drury did not apply until July 1915. To his surprise he was accepted at once and sent on a troop ship to Egypt. In Egypt he was mainly occupied in base and regional hospitals. He was very much his own boss and had to work out for himself a regime for work and hospital visiting. In January 1916 he became Chaplain to the Shoubreh Hospital and to the Military Police. Although working in Cairo he stayed in billets near the Turf Club and dined there nightly. This life, one stage removed from military regime, did not last long and Drury was attached to the London Brigade and quickly became initiated into military life, taking parade services and marching on night exercises. After a while with the regiment in Mesopotamia, it was sent to France, arriving on the Somme in June 1916. The 2/1 London Regiment was part of the diversionary arrack at Gommecourt and Drury worked with other chaplains such as the Revds Bickersteth and Palmer in the ambulance and casualty clearing stations.

In his book *Camp Follower* he related his experiences in the Somme Battle and how he got used to conducting services under machine gun fire and shelling. He recounts how he gradually learned pastoral techniques of relating to the men in battle situations:

> When we were in the trenches I used to pay a daily visit to the firing line. This had distinct advantages from the point of view of parish work. The bay of a firing trench was an ideal spot for a quiet talk, and the uncertainty of life made men readier to speak frankly of serious things.[16]

He met Studdert Kennedy and accompanied him on some burial parties. He was impressed by his belief that a padre should seek out the dangerous spots in order to counteract the idea that the chaplain had a soft job.

He was sent to relieve Bickersteth with the 2/1 London Ambulance and it was there that he was wounded in the jaw and arm.[17] On his recovery he was bitterly disappointed to learn on his return that he had been replaced as chaplain to the 1st London Regiment and when the opportunity arose he volunteered for duty in Mesopotamia. After a voyage taking in Africa and India he arrived in the Persian Gulf and onto Samara becoming Chaplain to the 101st RGA Brigade who were taking part in the push up the Tigris and on to Tikrit. He was present on 30 October 1918 at the surrender of the Ottoman armies. After the armistice he stayed in Mesopotamia, eventually arriving home in November 1919.

The Revd William Drury did not become a famous army chaplain or a post-war household name. He was not decorated for bravery and had not mentioned or spoken about the war until writing his memoirs in 1968.[18] His story, however, full of both the mundane and the dangerous aspects of a chaplain's life, puts into context the ordinary life of a padre in the Great War. It is probable that many chaplains like him did not concern themselves with the controversies of holy grocery or religious revival, but just got on, overwhelmed by the enormity of their task, often unsure of their role but concentrating above all on bringing the reality of God to the lives of men engaged in total war.

Revd Geoffrey Studdert Kennedy

'Woodbine Willie' as Studdert Kennedy became nicknamed, is the most contradictory and controversial figure among the army chaplains who became known during the Great War. He was full of contradictions, physically frail yet resistant and brave in battle. Down to earth, sometimes shocking and superficial in his sermons, yet thinking in a deeply theological manner in his writings. Jingoistic and supportive of the military cause in his talks, he was yet capable of writing poetry that showed his deep abhorrence of war and pity for the plight of the soldier caught up in it.

The Revd G. A. Studdert Kennedy, 'Woodbine Willie' (RAChD Archives)

He began his ministry as a chaplain in the railway sidings at Rouen, sending off drafts to the front. He used a mixture of singing, preaching and individual attention to troops, finally going on the train just before departure to distribute bibles and cigarettes. His talent as a preacher and his ability to hold the rapt attention of large crowds was soon recognised. The Revd D F Carey, a senior chaplain who got to know Studdert Kennedy very well, described his preaching – "Never once did he fail to hold their attention and inspire them with the big things in life."[19] Some of his addresses were published in *Rough Talks by a Padre* and he was selected to be one of the speakers who publicised the National Mission of Repentance and Hope to the army in France. His periods of time at the front were spent being as close as possible to the front line. He won an MC at Messines in 1917 – "For conspicuous gallantry and devotion to duty. He showed the greatest courage and disregard for his own safety in attending to wounded."[20] His experience in the front line resulted in his poetry, written in soldiers' vernacular 'Rough Rhymes' as well as other conventional poetry evoking the life at the front.

His career as a chaplain touches on all the controversies that have been spawned by a consideration of the chaplain's role. He has been accused of being too much in the pockets of the military regime and of paying too much attention to the wishes of the generals. He has been thought to characterise the chaplains' role as being too much one of bringing material comfort to the troops. He had, at the heart of his ministry however, the bravery to go with his men into battle and to have a clear awareness of what was necessary to achieve an intimate relationship with them, both by his physical presence, bearing cigarettes, and his spiritual support. William Drury remembers him speaking to a group of chaplains at St Omer. "He urged us chaplains to seek the most dangerous positions, as our presence was the best expression we could give of our message to the troops."[21] He summed up his personal philosophy of his role as a chaplain. "You can pray with them sometimes but pray for them always."[22] His career in the war certainly raised the profile of Army Chaplains then and in subsequent years.

Revd Theodore Bayley Hardy

Although many chaplains faced danger in the frontline, Bayley Hardy stands out clearly as a priest of exemplarily courage. His actions in battle were the result of an acute

The Revd T. Bayley Hardy receiving the Victoria Cross from King
George V at Frohen–le-Grande, August 1918. (IWM Q11128)

understanding of the pressure felt by men in the front line and a straightforward and determined approach to the ways in which a chaplain could best serve his men.

Theodore Bayley Hardy was born in 1863 and during a 10-year career as a teacher, he contemplated whether he should be ordained. He took this step in 1898. It is not surprising, given his attitude of all-encompassing care to men in the trenches, that one of the reasons he delayed ordination so long was his dislike of some of the damnatory clauses in the Athenasian Creed. After a career as a headmaster, he took up a living in Hutton Roof, Westmorland, in order to spend more time with his wife during her final illness. She died in June 1914. He decided to join up as an army chaplain but because of his age, 51, he was not successful in his application until 1916. His biographer, David Raw, says of him "Theodore Hardy knew with instinctive certainty that the front line was the place where he ought to be. When he got there he was to demonstrate by action as much as words what that certainty meant."[23] In a well-documented and famous meeting with Studdert Kennedy, Hardy was impressed with the idea of living with the men. Studdert Kennedy encouraged him "Work in the front and they will listen to you when they come out to rest, but if you only preach and teach behind you are wasting your time … The men will forgive you for anything but lack of courage and devotion. Without that you are useless."[24]

Like many chaplains, Bayley Hardy had to serve his apprenticeship at base camp before being moved up to the line. In March 1917 he was at Arras and moved up to the Ypres salient in June where he was to stay until March 1918. David Raw explains how, after disappointments with attendance at voluntary services, Hardy decided to live entirely with the officers and men of the line. It was at Lens that his first recorded act of heroism took place, that of bringing a wounded man down from the 'Double Crassier' under fire and with unsafe conditions underfoot. An incident at Oosterverne in April 1917 resulted in him being awarded the DSO. He stayed with a soldier, who was dying, up to his neck with mud and slime. Hardy himself had a broken arm but stayed with the soldier until he died and then read the burial service over him. In the attack at Passchendaele in October, Hardy continued his policy of organising stretcher parties to rescue men in No Man's Land resulting in an action that won him the MC.

When his own battalions were relieved, Hardy would stay in the front line with the relieving battalion, being "handed over as a trench store."[25] It was on the Somme at Rossignol Wood, in the battles resulting from the German offensive of March 1918 that Bayley Hardy won his VC. He had stayed all day near an enemy machine gun post attending a wounded man and emerged at dusk to get help to bring him in and then continued his work among the wounded under fire. The citation for his VC mentions three separate acts of bravery and says "He has by his fearlessness, devotion to the men of his battalion and quiet unobtrusive manner, won the respect and admiration of the whole division."[26] King George V presented his VC to him on 3 August 1918 at Army HQ, Frohen le Grand.

By April 1918 pressure was being put upon him by the King and the church authorities to return home. He was offered a lucrative living in the Fells but felt that it was his duty to remain at the front, and also that when he did return he owed it to the parishioners of Hutton Roof to return to them. He did not, however, make that return. In the first week of October his Leicesters' and Somersets' were pursuing the retreating Germans near the banks of the River Selle. Bayley Hardy was wounded in the thigh, brought in by stretcher-bearers but died a week after being wounded on 15 October. The Revd Vallings, his friend throughout much of his time at the front said that Hardy looked upon his wife as alive to him, in constant communion and fellowship. "He believed that he could not do better, if God so willed, than to join his beloved wife in the presence of the Lord."[27]

Bayley Hardy's attitude to his role in the trenches is illustrative of much of the ideas discussed in this book. He understood the importance of comradeship and sharing experiences with the troops, but was not afraid to be the bearer of cigarettes and material comforts as well a spiritual comfort. He set great store by saying the funeral service over his soldiers even under heavy fire and advised shortening the period of preparation for confirmation so that men could receive Holy Communion. He was the same to every man, appearing in the trenches with his trademark expression "It's only me" and was non-judgemental in his attitude towards men of all ranks. He was not a rabble-rouser or an encourager of hatred of the Germans. He taught that the enemy was not to be hated and that with love and mercy come reconciliation. He cannot be accused of encouraging the men to fight the Germans under the auspices of God's war. He concentrated on bringing God's comfort to men by his presence in the front line.

Notes

1. Alan Wilkinson, *The Church of England in the First World War*, p. 127.
2. Leighton Green, *Somewhere in Flanders*, p. 30.
3. F. Barry, *Period of my Life*, p. 59.
4. L.H. Gwynne, Diaries and papers (XACC/18/F/1, XACC/18/Z/1).
5. Ibid.
6. H. Blackburne, *This also Happened on the Western Front*, p. 62.
7. Barry, op. cit., p. 58.
8. Ibid, p. 59.
9. Ibid.
10. Wilkinson, op.cit., p. 127.
11. S. Louden, *Chaplains in Conflict*, p. 47.
12. H.L. Gwynne, *Royal Army Chaplains' Department Quarterly Journal*, No 5, January 1923 (Vol 2).
13. Ibid.
14. Barry, op. cit., p. 60.
15. Ibid, p. 59.
16. Drury, op.cit., p. 116.
17. Service record of the Revd W Drury, National Archives (WO39/11055).
18. Letter from Mr C. Jeanes, Church Organist, Parish of Wilton.
19. J.K.Mozley, *G.A. Studdert Kennnedy by his Friends*, p. 129.
20. Ibid, p. 143.
21. Drury, op. cit., p. 127.
22. Carey, op, cit., p. 141.
23. David Raw, *It's Only Me, Life of Theodore Bayley Hardy*, p. 16.
24. Ibid, p. 21.
25. Ibid, p. 61.
26. Ibid, p. 77.
27. Ibid, p. 83.

Conclusion

An assessment of how the Anglican Chaplains who served in the Great War coped with the challenge and difficulties of their position involves an examination of the criticisms that have been levelled at them and a consideration of criteria by which they are to be judged. Criticisms include their inability to relate to the troops, their controversial role as morale boosters, their efforts as entertainment officers and refreshment providers and the allegations about the effectiveness of their role in battle. The bad press that chaplains received has to a large extent influenced subsequent generations of historians and the public's view of the performance of the chaplains in the Great War. In the same manner that revisionist historians have rehabilitated the reputation of the generals, recent research by historians such as Michael Snape, Richard Schweitzer and Duff Crerar has provided a wider, less stereotypical image of the Church of England at war.

In November 1916 the Revd Neville Talbot wrote *Thoughts on Religion at The Front*, in which he tried to make sense of the role of the church and the chaplains in the war and to look at the ways in which religion was part of the soldier's life at the front. A comment in his second chapter sums up much of the difficulty experienced by chaplains in their role:

> There is something wrong about the status of chaplains. They belong to what the author of *A Student in Arms* calls the 'super world of officers', which is separate from the men. ... We are in an unchristian position, in the sense that we are in a position which Christ would not have occupied. He, I'm sure would have been a regimental stretcher bearer, truly among and of the men.[1]

Many of the Anglican Chaplains struggled with ways in which to become closer to the men they served, and much of the criticism levelled against them by Graves, Chapman and other post – war writers is based on the sometimes misguided attempts of the chaplains to be 'one of the boys', to be overtly militaristic and not very spiritual. The gloss and sensationalism of celebrity books by such as Graves and Sassoon written to appeal to large audiences and make money, must be taken into account, with their consequent exaggerations of style and content. What are left are the facts about chaplains, in their words, in the opinions of contemporaries and in the evidence of their work.

Chaplains have been criticised by a number of individuals, not only by literary figures but also by church historians. As we have seen, Louden roundly criticizes the role of the chaplains in what he sees as propping up the military morale. Contemporary writers such as the Revd E C Crosse do no see such a difference in the work of supporting and ministering to the men and the supposed use of them by generals. He is transparent in his pleasure that the generals are appreciating the work of the chaplains, and he does not see their role as propping up discipline or war mongering, so much as making sure that men lived and died with the support and knowledge of God.

Chaplains such as Studdert Kennedy have been accused of undue bellicosity and militarism, using the word of God to encourage the military warfare machine. It is true that some chaplains did start the war in the same patriotic and bellicose mode that most of their contemporaries did. Their background and class surely condemned them to this. Many of them thought hard and thought again during wartime conditions and many found, as Crosse did, that there was no call for jingoistic or militaristic talk from padres in the trenches. Studdert Kennedy, although caught up in some official morale boosting, spent more time in worrying about the thoughts and pains of the ordinary soldier than encouraging them to fight. His poems show an intimate knowledge of the concerns and motivations of the ordinary soldier and also left the reader in no doubt about his views on the horror and wastefulness of war.

Another criticism of chaplains up until 1916, but which lingered throughout and long after the war, was that they were not up in the front line trenches in action like their Roman Catholic contemporaries. We have seen the reasons for this in that the orders from generals in the first part of the war were that padres got in the way and were to keep back from the front lines. The combination of pressure from chaplains and the realisation by high command that they could usefully boost morale resulted in the rescinding of that order. From then on senior chaplains formulated careful plans about the role of their chaplains in time of action. Harry Blackburne contributed well thought out instructions about where chaplains could be most useful in action. The actions of clergy depended on their physical position. As we have seen, chaplains based with medical units were by no means in 'cushy' positions and performed many brave deeds. There is also no doubt that the more the chaplain could get into the front line and give support to the troops, the more they respected him. The actions of the Revds Mellish, Hardy and Peel certainly proved that chaplains could be very brave, but were echoed in the many more injuries and decorations received by chaplains carrying in wounded under fire.

The controversy about 'Holy Grocery', that is whether chaplains were right to concentrate much of their efforts on providing for the physical comfort of their troops, is one that perplexed chaplains at the time and has caused controversy since. Once again the chaplains are in an untenable position. If they didn't bother with material comforts they would be described as standoffish and too spiritual. Trying to provide both material and spiritual comforts, they were criticised for neglecting the religious part of their job. Similar problems have been felt in the church ever since and are part of the tensions of the church working in society. Is its job to proclaim the Kingdom of God solely in worship or has it a duty to be involved in the social and economic problems of the parish and nation?

There is no doubt that the chaplains strove mightily to provide services to all the troops at the front. A contemporary criticism, voiced in the national press and in the Church Times, was that the chaplains were thinly spread or congregated in the wrong places.[2] There was persistent discussion about the efficiency and scope of recruitment of chaplains and controversy later in the war about the possibility of call-up. Bishop Gwynne pressed strongly for this but Archbishop Davidson preferred a more indirect approach to individuals via his 'Lambeth scheme', the compilation of a list of interested or eligible clergy.[3] The necessity of clergy for the front was weighed against the reluctance of the bishops to denude their parishes of able clergy. Despite the difficulties chaplains did make heroic efforts to provide services, travelling many miles on Sundays and taking many services.

So by what criteria are the Anglican Chaplains to be judged? Their success in the fulfilling of material needs? Of providing adequate services? Their work with hospitals and ambulances? Of being with men in frontline battle? With hindsight it is easy to separate the multifarious tasks that were the lot of the wartime chaplain, but to him they were all of one woven piece. Providing physical and material help was not separated in the chaplain's mind from providing spiritual comfort in services and pastoral visits to the trenches. A chaplain's job was to minister to the men of the army in whatever way he could, regardless of the distinctions we would now impose on his different functions. If Jesus could heal the sick and provide food for the five thousand as well as proclaiming God's Kingdom then surely that was their job also.

Chaplains at the beginning of the war did not have a clearly defined role in the new concepts of mass trench warfare. In the same way as the commanders of the army had to learn new tactics so did the chaplains. Each chaplain had to define his own role in the job, depending on his individual skills and circumstances. Some concentrated on providing havens of material and spiritual comfort such as Talbot House; some found their niche in base hospitals and some in the front line trenches. Some ministered to material needs, some to spiritual, most to both. They were simply men of God in the maelstrom of war endeavouring to bring God to the lives of the men in the trenches in whatever way they could. They should be remembered as such.

Notes

1.   Neville Talbot, *Thoughts on Religion at the Front*, pp. 3-4.
2.   *The Church Times*, 1 October 1915, 21 January 1916, 22 October 1917.
3.   Michael Snape, *God and the British Soldier*, p. 184.

Bibliography

Archival sources

Church Missionary Society Archives, University of Birmingham
XACC/18/F/1 Diaries of L. H Gwynne
XACC/18/Z/1 Army Book

Imperial War Museum
87/10/1   R Bulstrode
80/22/1   E C Crosse
78/7/1   M Evers
90/7/1   C I S Hood
80/22/1   L Jeeves
77/10/71   T G Rogers
1/51/94   H Spooner

National Archives
War Diary, Principal Chaplain (WO/95/2023).
War Diary, Senior Chaplain 8th Division (WO 95/2023).
War Diary, 55th Field Ambulance (WO95/2030).
War Diary 54th Field Ambulance (WO95/2031).

Royal Army Chaplains' Department, Amport House
The Papers of the Very Revd H W Blackburne, D S O, M C.
General Horne, 'An address to the Chaplains, 1st Corps', 6 March 1916.

Journals and Newspapers

The Church Times newsapaper, 1914-18
The Times newspaper, 1914-18
The following articles from the *Quarterly Journal of the Royal Army Chaplains' Department*:
  The Bishop of Lahore, 'The R.A.Ch. D in Mesopotamia', Vol 2 No 7 (July 1923), pp.266-268.
  Bishop L. H. Gwynne, No 5, Jan 1923, Vol 2.
  The Revd Duncan Blair MC DD, 'Leaves From the Journal of a Scottish Padre in the First World War', No 8 June 1954 Vol 18, pp 44-50.
  The Revd Horsley Smith, 'A Chaplain's Recollections of 1917-18'. December 1978, Vol 24, pp 19-25.
Wilkinson, A., 'The Paradox of the Military Chaplain', *Theology*, 1984, pp. 249-57.

Printed books

Arthur, M., *Forgotten Voices of the Great War*, London, Ebury Press, 2003.

Barry, F.R., *Period of my Life*, London, Hodder & Stoughton, 1970.

Bickersteth, J. (ed.), *The Bickersteth Diaries*, London, Leo Cooper, 1995.

Blackburne, H.W., *This also happened on the Western Front. The padre's story*, London, Hodder & Stoughton, 1932.

Brabant, F.H., *Neville Stuart Talbot 1879-1943: A Memoir*, London, SCM Press, 1949.

Brown, M., *1918: Year of Victory*, London, Pan, 1998.

Cairns, Revd D.S., (ed), *The Army and Religion*, London, Macmillan, 1919.

Chapman, G., *A Passionate Prodigality. Fragments of Autobiography*, London, Buchan & Enright, 1985.

Clayton, P., *Tales of Talbot House. Everyman's Club in Poperinghe and Ypres 1915-1918*, London, Chatto & Windus, 1919.

Crerar, D., *Padres in No Man's Land. Canadian Chaplains and the Great War*, Montreal and Kingston, McGill-Queens University Press, 1995.

Creighton, O., *With the Twenty-Ninth Division in Gallipoli*, London, Longmans, 1916.

Drury, W., *Camp Follower*, private publication, 1968.

Dunn, J.C., *The War the Infantry Knew 1914-1919 : a chronicle of service in France and Belgium with the Second Battalion, His Majesty's Twenty-third Foot, the Royal Welch Fusiliers founded on personal records, recollections and reflections*, London, P. King, 1938.

Graham, S., *Private in the Guards*, London, Macmillan, 1919.

Graves, R., *Goodbye to All That: An Autobiography*, London, Penguin, 1999.

Hankey, D., *A Student in Arms*, London, Andrew Melrose, 1916.

Holmes, R., *Tommy: the British soldier on the Western Front 1914-1918*, London, Harper, 2004.

Horne, J. (comp.), *The Best of Good Fellows: the diaries and memoirs of the Rev. Charles Edmund Doudney, M.A., C.F. (1871-1915)*, London, Jonathon Horne Publications, 1995.

Jackson, H.C., *Pastor on the Nile: Being some account of the life and letters of Llewellyn H. Gwynne*, London, SPCK, 1960.

Kennedy, E.J., *With the Immortal Seventh Division*, London, Hodder and Stoughton, 1915.

Langston, E. L., *Bishop Taylor Smith*, Edinburgh, Marshall Morgan & Scott, 1939.

Lever, T., *Clayton of Toc H*, London, John Murray, 1971.

Lloyd, Roger, *The Church of England 1900-1965*, SCM Press, 1966.

Lockhart, J. G., *Cosmo Gordon Lang*, London, Hodder & Stoughton, 1949.

Louden, S., *Chaplains in Conflict: the role of army chaplains since 1914*, London, Avon Books, 1996.

Maclaren, S. J., (ed.), *Somewhere in Flanders*, The Lark's Press, 2005.

Maclean Watt, L., *In France and Flanders with the Fighting Men*, London, Hodder & Stoughton, 1917.

Macnutt, B., (ed.), *The Church in the Furnace: essays by seventeen temporary Church of England Chaplains on active service in France and Flanders*, London, Macmillan, 1918.

Mozley, J.K., et. al., *G.A. Studdert Kennedy. By his friends*, London, Hodder and Stoughton, 1929.

Prentice, S., *Padre*, New York, Dutton, 1919.

Pym, T. W. and Gordon, G., *Papers From Picardy*, Boston and New York, Houghton Mifflin, 1917.

Raw, D., *It's Only Me. Life of Theodore Bayley Hardy*, Gatebeck, Peters, 1988.

Richards, F., *Old Soldiers Never Die*, Uckfield, Naval & Military Press, 2001.

Schweitzer, R., *The Cross and the Trenches: religious faith and doubt among British and American Great War soldiers*, Wesport, Connecticut, Praeger, 2003.

Smyth, J.G., *In this Sign Conquer. The Story of the Army Chaplains*, Oxford, Mowbray, 1968.

Snape, M., *God and the British Soldier: Religion and the British Army in the First and Second World Wars*, Abingdon, Routledge, 2005.

Snape, M., *The Royal Army Chaplains' Department 1796-1953: Clergy under fire*, Woodbridge, The Boydell Press, 2008.

Talbot, N., *Thoughts on Religion at the Front*, London, Macmillan, 1917.

White, J., *With the Cameronians in France: Leaves from a Chaplain's diary*, Glasgow, John Smith & Son, 1915.

Wilkinson, A., *The Church of England in the First World War,* London, SCM Press, 1978.

Winnifrith.D.P., *The Church in the Fighting Line,* London, Hodder & Stoughton, 1915.

Index

Related titles published by Helion & Company

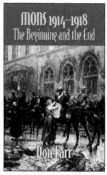

Mons 1914-1918:
The Beginning and the End
Don Farr
232pp   Hardback
ISBN 978-1-906033-28-6

*Most Unfavourable Ground:
the Battle of Loos 1915*
Niall Cherry
380pp   Paperback
ISBN 978-1-906033-21-7

A selection of forthcoming titles:

*The Other Side of the Wire Volume One: With the German XIV Reserve Corps
on the Somme, September 1914–June 1916*
R.J. Whitehead
ISBN 978-1-906033-29-3

*The Silent General: Horne of the First Army.
A Biography of Haig's Trusted Great War Comrade-in-Arms*
Don Farr
ISBN 978-1-906033-47-7

*Sniping in France 1914-18: With Notes on the
Scientific Training of Scouts,Observers, and Snipers*
Major H. Hesketh-Prichard DSO MC
ISBN 978-1-906033-49-1

HELION & COMPANY
26 Willow Road, Solihull, West Midlands B91 1UE, England
Telephone 0121 705 3393   Fax 0121 711 4075
Website: http://www.helion.co.uk